DRAGONFLIES

· WILD GUIDE ·
DRAGONFLIES

595.733 pb

Cynthia Berger

illustrations by Amelia Hansen
and Michigan Science Art

STACKPOLE
BOOKS

$19.95

4-04

Published by
STACKPOLE BOOKS
5067 Ritter Road
Mechanicsburg, PA 17055
www.stackpolebooks.com

Printed in China

10 9 8 7 6 5 4 3 2 1

First edition

Cover design by Caroline Stover
Species account watercolors by Amelia Hansen
All other illustrations by Michigan Science Art:
  Joseph E. Trumpey, director
  Wendy Baker
  Emily S. Damstra
  Barbara Duperron
  Patricia Ferrer
  Gillian Harris
  Jonathan Higgins
  Jacqueline Mahannah
  Michelle L. Meneghini
  Bruce Worden

Library of Congress Cataloging-in-Publication Data

Berger, Cynthia.
    Dragonflies / Cynthia Berger ; illustrations by Amelia Hansen and the Michigan Science Art Group.
        p.   cm.
    ISBN 0-8117-2971-0
    1. Dragonflies.   I. Title.
QL520 .B457   2004
595.7'33—dc22

2003022285

CONTENTS

ACKNOWLEDGMENTS

I owe a very large "thank you" to Mark F. O'Brien, coordinator of collections in the insect division of the Museum of Zoology at the University of Michigan. Mark served as the technical editor for this book; he patiently answered my many dragonfly questions, reviewed the final manuscript for accuracy, and worked closely with all of the illustrators involved with the project. His knowledge of and enthusiasm for all things odonate is inspiring.

I'm also very grateful to Clark Shiffer of State College, Pennsylvania, retired wildlife biologist with the Pennsylvania Fish and Boat Commission, who let me tag along for some dragonfly-watching at his favorite meadow, helped me narrow down the list of species to be covered in the field guide section, and provided feedback on the final manuscript.

Thanks are due to Rutgers University entomology professor Michael May for filling me in on his fascinating research into dragonfly thermoregulation and migration. Sidney Dunkle, a biology professor at Collin County Community College, Spring Creek Campus, in Plano, Texas, and the author of *Dragonflies through Binoculars*, had all the answers to all my questions about the etymology of dragonfly names. Kathy Biggs, the author of *Common Dragonflies of California*; Bob Glotzhober, Curator of Natural History for the Ohio Historical Society; and Craig Tufts, Chief Naturalist with the National Wildlife Federation, generously shared the tales of their adventures in creating backyard ponds to attract dragonflies.

Special thanks go to my editor at Stackpole Books, Mark Allison, for encouragement throughout the project, and also to Joyce Bond for her thoughtful editing.

I owe my interest in the natural world to my parents Jay and Kitty Berger. My husband, Bill Carlsen, has always supported my interest in aquatic insects. (When I was a graduate student—before we were married—he used to show up with a bunch of roses in one hand and a bucketful of mayfly nymphs in the other.)

The information presented here was painstakingly gathered by generations of scientists who have made the study of dragonflies their life's work. I hope this presentation of their combined wisdom will help to inspire wider interest in an ancient and fascinating insect group.

INTRODUCTION

Back in the late 1980s, I was working in Ithaca, New York, for *Living Bird*, a glossy quarterly published by the Cornell Laboratory of Ornithology. A typical issue of the magazine includes reports on bird research, lyrical essays about the joys of bird-watching, tips on species identification, and reviews of new bird-watching gear.

Like every magazine, *Living Bird* gets unsolicited story proposals from writers. One day, the mail brought us a proposal that was a little surprising. Animal behavior expert John Alcock of Arizona State University wanted to write a story for us, not about birds, but about damselflies.

The idea sounded so offbeat, we almost dismissed it out of hand. We didn't think a bug story would fly with *Living Bird* readers—the sort of bird-watchers described as "avid," the kind who own German binoculars costing more than the average mortgage payment, who use professional database software to manage their lengthy lists of bird sightings . . . who, if they think of insects at all, think of them as bird chow.

But finally, in our editorial meeting, we conceded that Alcock had a point. Bird-watchers, he argued, would be intrigued by these creatures because damselflies and their close relatives dragonflies, both members of the order Odonata, are a lot like birds. They fly around, they're big enough that you notice them, and you can watch them through binoculars. Lots of them come in bright, jewel-toned colors, and even the plain brown ones are aesthetically pleasing in shape. Like falcons and flycatchers, they are expert aerial predators capable of making dramatic captures in midair. Like Black-headed Grosbeaks and Red-winged Blackbirds, the males will often defend territories and jealously guard their mates. Like warblers and waterfowl, some species make seasonal migrations.

One last way in which dragonflies are like birds, said Alcock, is this: What facts we know about them—their distribution, abundance, and habits—we know in large part because of the work of amateurs, not scientists. North

American bird-watchers have been gathering information on bird population trends for more than a century through various citizen-science projects, such as the National Audubon Society's annual Christmas Bird Count. Dragonfly-watching has a shorter history as a popular hobby in North America (it's long been popular in Great Britain), but in just the past decade, a number of states have launched annual dragonfly surveys conducted by amateur enthusiasts. More often than you might think, survey participants locate species never before sighted in a state or discover that a species thought to be rare is actually widespread or commonplace. Making careful field notes and keeping track of species sighted, bird-watchers and dragonfly-watchers both play key roles in adding to the sum total of scientific knowledge.

With these similarities in mind, we decided to run Alcock's bug story in our bird magazine. And readers responded enthusiastically. Meanwhile, once I'd had my consciousness raised about dragonflies, I started paying more attention to them. On birding trips, I noticed my binoculars were straying from the feathered fliers to their four-winged counterparts.

That was more than a decade ago. These days, I'm not the only one on birding trips sneaking peeks at dragonflies. Dragonflies are "in." In home decor, they've surpassed butterflies and ladybugs as the most popular insect on fabrics and ornaments. North American dragonfly field guides have been published, as have a number of state guides, with more in the works. Three states—Washington, Alaska, Michigan—have chosen dragonflies as their official state insect. There are even enough Odonata enthusiasts—or "Odo-nuts," as some call themselves—to support annual Dragonfly Festivals in Texas and New Mexico.

Today it's easier for amateurs to follow their passion and study dragonflies. Just a few decades ago, only a few species had common names like birds and butterflies and wildflowers do; if you wanted to identify a dragonfly you spotted flying around a local wetland, you needed a working knowledge of Latin. In 1978, the Dragonfly Society of the Americas (DSA) developed a unified system for assigning common names to odonates. Since then, the system has been improved and updated several times. The new dragonfly names are eminently logical, based on obvious traits or habits. For example, the Twelve-spotted Skimmer has twelve bold spots on its wings, and Beaverpond Basket-tails and Seaside Dragonlets can be found right where their names suggest. Some dragonfly names are delightfully poetic: there are Shadowdragons, Boghaunters, Firetails, and Sprites, to name just a few.

The development of close-focusing binoculars has also boosted the sport of dragonfly-watching. Conventional binoculars are designed to help you see things that are far away. The new close-focusing models, engineered with bird-watchers in mind but excellent for dragonfly- and butterfly-watching as well, give you a crisp, clear, magnified view of creatures that are close at hand, such as a dragonfly perched a few yards away on a stem of meadow grass.

Another recent innovation has been the development of user-friendly field guides. No longer do beginners have to struggle with ponderous academic tomes that require you to investigate the shape of the genitalia in order to identify a species. Two guides especially worth noting are *Dragonflies through Binoculars*, by Sidney W. Dunkle, and the *Beginner's Guide to Dragonflies*, by Blair Nikula, Jackie Sones, and Donald and Lillian Stokes. Dunkle's work is a guide to all 307 dragonfly species (not, however, damselflies) found in North America. The Stokes guide is a pocket-size introduction to about 100 of the most common North American damselfly and dragonfly species. You don't need an advanced degree in entomology to use these new field guides, which employ both common and scientific names and have lots of color photographs.

This book is an introductory guide for all the other bird-watchers who have turned their binoculars to dragonflies, and for anyone else who is intrigued by these glittering aerial acrobats. If you are just beginning to take a closer look at dragonflies and you want to learn more about their habits and haunts, this book will get you started. Once you're hooked, the Resources section tells you where to go for more information. Lists of field guides, reference books, helpful websites, and dragonfly organizations are provided.

Happy dragonflying!

1

Jeweled Acrobats

Visit any small pond on a sunny midsummer afternoon, and you'll see the surface of the water alive with dragonflies. If you watch for a while, the first thing you'll notice is how many different kinds there are. Some are as large as hummingbirds, others are as small as flies. Some are dull brown or black, others have glittering metallic bodies, and still others are jewel-toned. Some have transparent wings that seem to glitter in the sun; others have brightly colored wings like butterflies.

These varied dragonflies will be doing many different things. By the shore, males may patrol their territories with military precision or skirmish with competitors. Over open water, females swoop to lay their eggs, touching their abdomens daintily to the surface. Hot and thirsty dragonflies splash down to the water's surface to drink. Hungry dragonflies dart and wheel, grabbing gnats and mosquitoes on the wing. The pace is frenetic, the surface of the pond like a circus ring full of tumbling acrobats.

Scientists count about 6,500 species of dragonflies alive worldwide today—at least, that's the count so far. You can find dragonflies almost everywhere in the world that you find fresh water. They live on every continent except Antarctica.

Though this may sound like a lot of species, the insect order Odonata, made up of the dragonflies and damselflies, is a comparatively small group. Consider that the insect order Hymenoptera—the bees, wasps, and ants—has about 100,000 species. The insect order Lepidoptera—butterflies and moths—has twice that many, about 200,000 species in all. And the largest order, the Coleoptera, or beetles, has at least 300,000 and possibly as many as 500,000 species.

With 6,500 named species worldwide, dragonflies are comparable in diversity to birds, of which about 9,600 named species are known. Dragonflies are a small enough group that an enthusiast can, with diligence, search out and see a good-size subset. In North America, there are about 425 species of dragonflies—a manageable number for a budding dragonfly enthusiast to learn about—and additional species are still being discovered.

Dragonflies versus Damselflies

Scientists divide the 6,500 members of the insect order Odonata into two smaller suborders: the Anisoptera, or dragonflies, and the Zygoptera, or damselflies.

How can you tell the difference between dragonflies and damselflies? Dragonflies tend to be big and stocky, whereas damselflies tend to be little and dainty, though there are a few exceptions to this rule. Also, adult dragonflies and damselflies hold their wings in different ways when perched. Most damselflies fold their wings together and hold them erect above the back, butterfly-style. A perched damselfly looks like a small boat with a single sail hoisted. Dragonflies lack the anatomical "hinges" that allow damselflies to fold their wings above the back. Instead, they perch the way moths do—with their wings spread flat, like the pages of an open book.

You also can tell dragonflies from damselflies by the way they fly. Dragonflies tend to be strong, fast fliers, and their flight appears purposeful, directed. Damselflies look weak and a little aimless in flight; they are more likely to flit and flutter. Another way to tell a damsel from a dragon is to look closely at the insect's head while it is perched and note the placement of the eyes. A damselfly's eyes are usually positioned on the sides of the head, well separated from one another. Dragonflies, in contrast, tend to have eyes that are closely spaced—so close that they touch, or nearly touch, one another.

Dragonflies and damselflies are also easy to tell apart as nymphs. Members of the two groups have different kinds of gills, the structures used for taking in oxygen underwater. Damselfly nymphs have external gills located on the tip of the abdomen—three plumelike extensions that look like a tiny rooster's tail. Dragonfly nymphs lack these feathery extensions. Instead, a dragonfly nymph's body ends in three short spines. The gills are hidden inside the abdomen.

The terminology can get a little confusing, as the name dragonfly can be used to mean all the odonates, both Anisoptera *and* Zygoptera, but it is often used in a narrower sense, to mean only the members of the suborder Anisoptera, and *not* the damselflies. In this book, the term dragonfly is used in both ways, but it should be clear from the context which use is intended.

Dragonfly Characteristics

As members of the insect order Odonata, dragonflies share certain traits that distinguish them from the other insect orders—traits that make dragonflies different from, say, the butterflies and moths; the bees, wasps, and ants; or the beetles.

The Northern Bluet (top) is a typical damselfly; it has a slender body and folds its wings together over its back when it perches. The Slaty Skimmer (bottom), a typical dragonfly, has a stocky body and perches with its wings flat, like an open book.

Damselflies are smaller, slimmer, and daintier-looking than dragonflies, not only as adults, but also as nymphs. Dragonfly and damselfly nymphs also differ in their underwater breathing apparatuses. Notice how the damselfly nymph on the bottom (an Ebony Jewelwing) has external gills—three feathery extensions at the tip of the abdomen. Dragonfly nymphs, such as the Common Green Darner at the top, have gills inside the abdomen.

Adult Dragonfly Anatomy

All dragonflies are insects, and all share typical insect characteristics. Each one has an external skeleton, or exoskeleton—a collection of hard plates made of a substance called chitin that are connected to one another by narrow, flexible membranes. Each has a body that is divided into three parts—the head, thorax, and abdomen.

The dragonfly's comparatively large, round head is its sensory processing center. On the head are two large compound eyes and three small, simple eyes

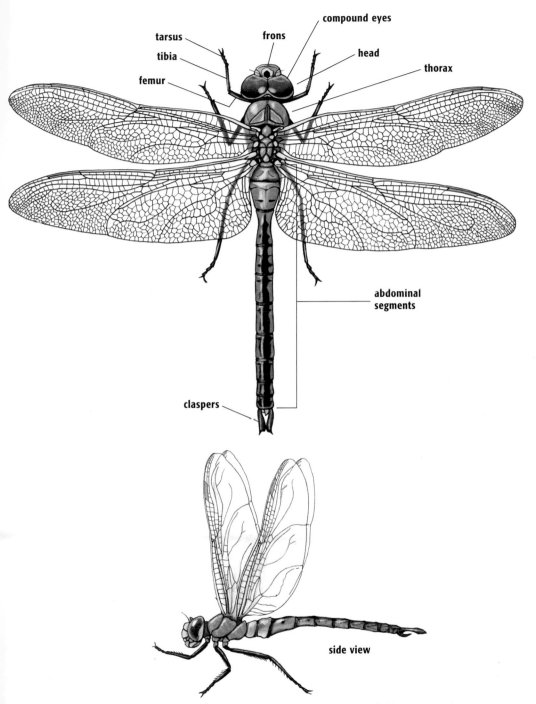

tarsus

frons

compound eyes

tibia

head

femur

thorax

abdominal
segments

claspers

side view

This male Common Green Darner shows the traits characteristic of all insects: a three-part body with a head, thorax, and abdomen; two pairs of wings; and three pairs of legs.

called ocelli. One distinctive dragonfly feature is its sharply serrated lower jaw, useful for seizing prey. This toothy jaw is what gives dragonflies the name Odonata, from the Greek meaning "toothed ones." Also on the head is a pair of very small, inconspicuous antennae. Jewelry designers and artists often depict dragonflies with large antennae, but that's a mistake. In the field, the small antennae are very hard to see.

The thorax is the dragonfly's power center. This is where the legs and wings attach to the body. All dragonflies have three pairs of legs and two pairs of narrow, transparent wings that can beat independently of one another. Veins in the wings transport hemolymph, the dragonfly equivalent of blood, and serve as air ducts and nerve conduits. They also stiffen and strengthen the wings. The large vein parallel to the leading edge of each wing is called the costa. The place where the costa joins other large veins, visible as a little indentation in the wing, is the nodus. This indentation helps the wing twist in flight. At the tip of each wing is a stigma, a blood-filled blister that looks like a solid rectangular spot.

The third part of the body, after the head and thorax, is the long, narrow abdomen. Despite its stiff, needlelike appearance, a dragonfly's abdomen is surprisingly flexible. In some situations, a dragonfly may curl its abdomen up over its back like a scorpion or under its thorax like a crayfish.

Nymph Anatomy

Before dragonflies become adults, they are known as nymphs. At this stage they look like different insects altogether, and lead very different lives. They have no functional wings. They do not fly. They don't even breathe air. Most nymphs live underwater—in ponds, lakes, rivers, streams, marshes, swamps, seeps, and springs. (In a few dragonfly species, the nymphs live not in liquid water, but in very moist environments, such as decaying leaves.)

In their appearance, nymphs make a striking contrast to the jewel-toned adults. Their bodies are shades of dull brown-black. They crawl. (Adult dragonflies never use their legs to walk anywhere—they only fly or perch.) And they breathe through gills.

All nymphs share a characteristic feature, one that is unique to dragonflies among all insects. The lower jaw, or labium, is more than a simple chewing mouthpart; it is a prehensile, dexterous appendage, a structure that works like an extra arm. Most of the time, a nymph's labium is folded flat against its face. But when the nymph goes after insect prey, it uses the labium like a speargun. When the nymph sights prey within reach, its labium shoots forward like a well-aimed missile, and moveable hooks on the front edge grab the flesh of the prey, be it a snail, tadpole, stonefly larva, or another dragonfly nymph. With this formidable weapon, nymphs can snatch prey as far as half a body length away. When the labium retracts, the prey is pulled into the nymph's waiting mouth.

2

A Year in the Life of a Dragonfly

Bird-watchers chart the progress of the seasons by what's flying at their favorite birding spots. Migratory species wing their way north from southern wintering grounds in spring. From Red-winged Blackbirds and warblers to waterfowl and shorebirds, each species shows up at a predictable time as spring progresses.

Dragonfly-watchers also mark the seasons by what's flying. As spring turns to summer, different dragonfly species appear around a local pond in a predictable sequence. A few species owe their sudden appearance to the fact that they are, like birds, migratory, arriving early in spring from southern wintering grounds. As with migratory birds, the adults breed; the young hatch out; and the next generation heads south for the winter in fall.

But for the most part, dragonflies don't have to travel in order to arrive on the local scene in spring. Most dragonflies are residents, present at local ponds, lakes, streams, and rivers all year round. So why do they show up only at certain times? The answer is that dragonflies exist in their familiar winged form for just a fraction of their total lifespan. They spend most of their lives as nymphs, living underwater, out of sight of human eyes. We only see them when they emerge from the water and take on their winged form.

Typically, temperate-zone dragonflies live for about a year, but they spend eleven months as nymphs, living underwater—and just one month as adults, flying around. A few North American species spend two, three, or even up to seven years as nymphs. You see dragonflies all summer because some take on their winged form early in spring, others later. But each individual lives as an adult for just a short time. After the adults mate and the females lay their eggs, dragonflies that aren't eaten by predators eventually die.

Most people, when they hear the word "dragonfly," think of the free-flying life-stage, but if you really want to understand the world of dragonflies, you need to take a close look at what they do all year round, especially during that long period of time when they're living underwater as nymphs.

In Greek mythology, the nymphs were a group of minor goddesses, all of them lovely young maidens. Different nymphs were associated with different habitats: There were tree nymphs, ocean nymphs, cloud nymphs, and naiads—nymphs who lived around streams, rivers, and lakes. You may even see some older reference books use the term naiad specifically to mean larval dragonflies.

Despite their evocative names, dragonfly nymphs don't look like enchanting young goddesses at all. They look ferocious. They have hard, armored bodies and jointed, spiderish legs. Their most distinctive feature is the large, prehensile lower lip, or labium. This mouthpart, unique to dragonflies among all insects, gives the nymphs a fierce, bulldoggish expression.

The term nymph is not reserved for immature dragonflies exclusively. Entomologists use this term to describe the early life stage in those insect species that undergo incomplete—as opposed to complete—metamorphosis.

In species that experience complete metamorphosis, there's a complete transformation, with the adult insect looking nothing like its earlier form, the larva (a winged butterfly bears the same relationship to a wormlike caterpillar). Species that undergo complete metamorphosis move through four life stages: egg, wormlike larva, pupa or cocoon, and adult.

Insects that experience incomplete metamorphosis have just three life stages: egg, nymph, and adult. And the nymph does resemble the adult. A dragonfly nymph may lack functional wings and live underwater, but it has the basic dragonfly body plan, with six legs and large eyes. There's no pupal stage—no butterfly chrysalis, no long period of quiet inactivity while body parts are rearranged. The nymph undergoes a series of molts, repeatedly shedding its skin as it grows larger and larger. In the final molt, it emerges as an adult.

Magical Metamorphosis

A water-dwelling dragonfly nymph turns into an air-breathing adult through a process called emergence. This transformation usually happens in spring or summer, and it happens amazingly fast, taking only about an hour.

A nymph "emerges" in two senses of the word. First it emerges from the water, perhaps by crawling up a cattail stem or some other support. Then it emerges from its old body. The hard outer skin splits open, and a winged dragonfly struggles out. Different dragonfly species emerge at different times, so—as with birds—you can chart the progress of the seasons by what species are flying around.

THE TIMING OF EMERGENCE

Temperate-zone dragonflies can be sorted into two groups, based on the timing of emergence: there are "spring species" and there are "summer species." Spring species emerge in March, April, or May. Summer species emerge later, in summer. The Emerald family includes many spring species, notably the widespread and easy-to-spot Common Baskettail. The Clubtail and Skimmer families include many summer species.

Spring and summer species differ in another important way. Among the spring species, members of a population tend to emerge in a rush. All the individuals in a given location will emerge at about the same time—usually within a one-week period. One day, for example, Springtime Darners are nowhere to be seen; the next day, they are everywhere. They mature, they find mates, the females lay eggs, and in a few weeks, it's all over. The flight season has ended. No more of these big, brown dragonflies hanging in the trees around streams and rivers. For the next eleven months, Springtime Darners will exist only as nymphs, concealed below the surface of the water.

In summer species, in contrast, the members of a population emerge over an extended period—a few individuals today, a few tomorrow, a few more next week, a few more the week after, and so on and so on, for weeks and weeks, and even for months. You could say the difference between a spring species and a summer species is like the difference between a college that sends out all of its acceptance letters on April 1 and a college with rolling admissions, where some new students show up at the start of every semester.

Scientists have concluded that spring species seem to enjoy certain advantages. For one thing, the sudden flush of dragonflies in spring confounds predators. Hungry birds and frogs gulp down tender new dragonflies like candy, but when the entire population emerges all at once, predators can't possibly consume every individual. So the chances are good that at least some dragonflies will survive to launch the next generation.

Spring species are also at an advantage when it's time to mate. With every member of the population reaching sexual maturity at the same time, it's comparatively easy to find a partner.

When you see summer species such as Swamp Darners around your local pond from May to September, it's easy to assume that you are seeing the same individuals all summer long—that these are very long-lived adult dragonflies. In fact, what you are seeing is just a case of constant turnover. New dragonflies are added to the population as the older ones complete their lifespans.

Just before a nymph is ready to emerge, its behavior changes. Like anyone who is about to embark on a transforming experience, it stops eating and gets very restless. Nymphs that have been spending their time in deep water head for shallow water at the edge of the pond, either by swimming or by crawling. Near shore, they find water plants or other supports and clamber upward, toward the surface. They poke their heads out into the air, and for a while, they just sit there, looking like tiny frogs squatting in the shallows. During this time, the nymph's respiratory system, which extracts oxygen from water, is

OBSERVING THE TRANSFORMATION

The transformation from nymph to adult happens so quickly that it can seem like magic. A closer look at the process reveals that—as with stage magic—advance preparation is the key.

If you keep nymphs in an aquarium, you may notice that they stop feeding a day or two before they are due to emerge. This is because the tissues that make up the large labium are being broken down and rearranged into the smaller mouthparts of an adult dragonfly.

Take a closer look, and you'll notice other preparations under way. The nymph's hard outer shell is semitransparent, and through it, you can see the growing wing buds enlarging. You can also see the large eyes of the adult dragonfly forming below the nymph's smaller ones. When these signs of changes are visible, you can be sure that within a few hours to a day or two, the nymphs will make their perilous ascent into a new world.

shutting down, while the adult's respiratory system, which extracts oxygen from air, is starting to work.

Actual emergence usually takes place under cover of darkness, either at night or in the early-morning hours. First the nymph climbs completely out of the water. Typically its ladder to the upper world is a cattail stem, reed, or other water plant, although some nymphs clamber up tree roots or trunks, rocks along the shoreline, or bridge abutments. They have even been known to take advantage of a handy human leg.

To emerge successfully, most dragonflies must perch with their bodies in a vertical position—head up and tail down (see pages 12 and 13, figure a). Members of the Clubtail family are an exception to this rule; they typically make their transformations while sitting horizontally on a flat surface such as a water lily leaf or a rock.

Whatever position a nymph requires in order to emerge, once it has chosen a suitable spot, it sinks its six sharp-clawed feet firmly into the substrate. The nymph may swing its body from side to side, perhaps testing its grip, or perhaps making sure it has plenty of room for the wings it is about to sprout. Then the nymph's skin starts to split down the back of the head (b). Slowly but steadily, the dragonfly tugs its body backward as it wiggles free of the old skin, starting with the head, then the thorax, then part of the abdomen.

At this point in the process, in most species, the emerging dragonfly does a sort of backbend, like a circus gymnast (c). Dangling head-down, with only the tip of its abdomen still inside the nymphal shell, the dragonfly rests for a moment while its new outer covering hardens with exposure to air. Then it curls back to an upright position, grips the old shell with its legs, and works the tip of its abdomen free of its confinement.

If you come across a dragonfly at this point in the emergence process, you will see what looks like two almost identical insects, perched close together (d, e). But one of them is just an empty shell. The new insect that clings near its former self doesn't look much like a dragonfly yet. Its abdomen is short and plump, not long and slender. Its wings don't really look like wings, just crumpled blobs of tissue.

But within minutes, the new dragonfly starts to swallow air and pump hemolymph, the dragonfly equivalent of blood, into its abdomen and wings, forcing them to expand to their full size (f). In less than an hour, the transformation is complete—almost.

The Adult Stage

Tenerals and Juveniles

Scientists have a special name for the freshly emerged dragonfly, resting on a plant stem: it is called a teneral, a term that comes from the Latin word for "tender" or "delicate." The new dragonfly *is* very soft and tender, with delicate coloring—it looks like a pale ghost of the sexually mature adult it will become. The bold, glittering colors of a typical adult dragonfly take time to develop.

Right now is a very dangerous stage in a dragonfly's life. Tenerals are weak, and they can't fly very well. Meanwhile, predators are everywhere. Fish, frogs, and spiders love to feast on the soft-bodied tenerals. So do many other dragonflies. Tenerals in spring make easy prey for birds that are feeding their newly hatched young. Many more tenerals die when they are knocked from their perches by boat wakes or sudden, stiff winds to drown in the water they once called home. Other tenerals succumb when the spring weather turns unusually cold or rainy.

It doesn't take long, however, for a teneral to gain enough strength to make its first flight. Small dragonflies may lift off as soon as half an hour after emerging. Larger species take a little longer to be flight-ready—from one to two hours. The newly airborne dragonflies head not, as you might expect, out over the ponds from which they emerged, but away from the water, toward the shelter of a woodland or a grassy meadow.

When they take flight, these new dragonflies leave behind exuviae—the hard exoskeletons that covered the emerging nymphs. Nymphs sink their claws so firmly into their emergence perches that exuviae may cling in place for days, weeks, or months before wind or rain sweeps them away. From a distance, these shells can fool you, as they closely resemble living nymphs climbing up the stems of cattails or reeds.

Dragonfly researchers often search deliberately for exuviae around a pond or wetland. The cast skins are a gold mine of information. From them, scientists can learn many things: what species of dragonflies are breeding in a particular body of water; how numerous each dragonfly species is; and the sex ratio, the number of males versus females in the population. That's a lot of information to be gleaned from discarded bits of skin—not to mention that counting exuviae is much easier and more convenient than trying to catch fast-flying adult dragonflies with an insect net.

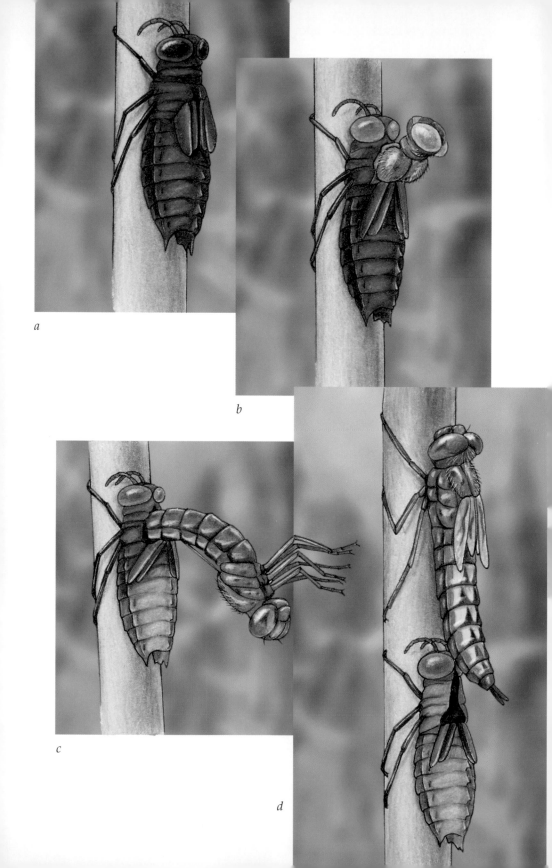

a

b

c

d

e

This series of images shows a Common Baskettail nymph making its final molt to become a winged, free-flying adult.

f

About twenty-four to forty-eight hours after emergence, the teneral dragonfly's body has hardened and developed some color. Now the dragonfly is considered a juvenile. Though more colorful than tenerals, juveniles are still not as colorful as they will be when they are sexually mature adults. The juveniles remain in their protected habitats—typically shady woodlands—for a week or two. During this time, they feed, bask in the sun, and fly around, developing muscles and gaining strength. It's a little like a spa vacation—heavy workouts and healthy food, getting in shape for the next stage of adult life.

Mature Adults

At the end of this period, the juvenile dragonfly's flight muscles are fully developed and its body is brightly colored. Now it is a sexually mature adult, ready to mate. The dragonfly leaves the shelter of the forest or field and heads for water—a lake, pond, puddle, bog or wetland, river or stream—whatever environment will provide appropriate habitat for the offspring it is about to produce.

Dragonflies that are ready to reproduce may go back to the body of water from which they emerged. But that's not necessarily true. Often dragonflies disperse, flying at random for a mile or two until they encounter a suitable body of water. This behavior is adaptive in the long term, because rivers can change course, and ponds come and go. A beaver dam may be breached; a lake may fill with sediment to become a marsh; flowing water may be stilled when a riverbend is cut off to form an oxbow lake. Dispersal behavior increases the chances that at least some members of a population will find good habitat in which to lay their eggs.

Around the water, adult males of some species establish feeding or breeding territories. Males can be aggressive in defending their turf, and their defensive behaviors are spectacular to watch. Members of the Skimmer family, in particular, are known for their territorial behavior. Members of the Darner family tend not to be territorial.

Now comes a brief period of intense activity, typically about two weeks but sometimes as long as a month, as males claim mates, couples copulate, and females lay their eggs.

Dragonfly Eggs

Each female dragonfly will likely mate several times over the course of her adult life, and after each mating she will lay a few hundred eggs. The eggs are microscopic—about the size of the period at the end of this sentence—and each has a tiny hole in one end. This is where the sperm enters, and also where the nymph hatches out.

Dragonfly eggs are typically either round or oval. Species that lay their eggs inside plant tissues—the damselflies, the petaltail dragonflies, and the darners—produce elongated, oval-shaped eggs. Most other species lay their eggs in water or some very wet place, and these species tend to lay round eggs.

Dragonflies that breed in rivers and streams lay eggs that are covered with a thin layer of sticky jelly, which helps the eggs cling to submerged plant leaves or stones rather than wash away downstream. For dragonflies that breed in ponds and lakes, losing eggs to the current isn't a problem. Pond species typically lay their eggs on the surface of the water, and the eggs then sink to the bottom. Eggs laid this way are very vulnerable to predation; you can sometimes spot small fish following a female dragonfly around a pond, eating the eggs as fast as they are laid. Eggs inserted in plant tissue, rotting wood, and similar materials are more protected. Among the species that hide their eggs, the females have sharp appendages on their abdomens, which they use to poke slits or holes for the eggs.

If a dragonfly's eggs escape predation, they typically hatch within a few days of being laid. In a few species, however, the eggs take longer to hatch. Spreadwing damselflies, in particular, tend to lay eggs that stay dormant all winter; they are laid in summer, but they don't hatch until the next spring.

The Nymph Stage

The tiny creature that hatches out of the pinhead-size egg is called a pronymph. Within a few seconds to a few hours after hatching, this tiny, almost featureless creature undergoes its first molt. It sheds its hard outer covering, and a slightly larger creature emerges—a six-legged nymph.

Most nymphs blend into their environment with camouflage colors, dark brown or very dark green, although there's some evidence that nymphs have the chameleonlike ability to change colors as they molt, adjusting the color of their exoskeletons to match the environment. In one laboratory experiment, nymphs that were reared in a glass aquarium with no sand or plants on the bottom changed colors as they molted, from dark to very pale.

Dragonfly nymphs molt repeatedly, and each time, the nymph emerges from its former skin in a body that is just a little bigger. The exact number of molts a dragonfly nymph must make to reach its full size varies from species to species. Among damselflies, nymphs in the Spreadwing family typically molt six to ten times, whereas Pond Damselfly nymphs molt nine to twelve times. Among dragonflies, nymphs in the Darner family typically undergo ten to thirteen molts; members of the Skimmer family molt less frequently.

The amount of time it takes for a nymph to complete its series of molts and be ready to emerge varies from species to species; it also depends on environmental conditions, including water temperature and food availability. In North America, most species take about eleven months to progress through their molts, though a few species speed through the process. Female Wandering Gliders, for example, lay their eggs in temporary puddles and ponds early in spring. The nymphs reach their full size, ready to emerge, in just forty days—with luck, before the puddle dries up. In contrast, nymphs of the massive clubtail called the Dragonhunter often take two years to complete their development. Dragonhunters lay their eggs in small, clear woodland streams, where food can be in short supply—part of the reason the nymphs tend to grow slowly. In the tropics, some species may spend five to seven years as nymphs before emerging.

There's no set interval between molts, either. The timing of each molt is influenced by such factors as how well the nymph has been eating and how warm the water is. Nymphs living in rivers heated by warm-water discharges from power plants grow faster than nymphs living in cooler water upstream. A Common Green Darner nymph living in a pond in Maine will take longer to reach full size than a darner in a pond in Georgia.

How Nymphs Breathe

Life in water is different from life on land in lots of ways, but one difference is very important: Water, not air, is the source of life-supporting oxygen. Adult dragonflies and damselflies take in air through spiracles, holes in the thorax and abdomen. Their nymphs can take in some oxygen by simple gas exchange through areas of the exoskeleton, much the way frogs absorb oxygen through moist skin. But for the most part, nymphs extract dissolved oxygen from water through their gills.

Damselflies and dragonflies have different kinds of gills. A damselfly's gills are on the outside of its body—three feathery structures protruding from the tip of the abdomen like a rooster's tailfeathers. Not only do these gills carry out gas exchange, but they can also work like paddles to propel the nymph through the water. Dragonfly nymphs, on the other hand, don't have visible gills; instead, the gills are hidden inside the rectal chamber. A nymph breathes through its anus: It "inhales" by using its abdominal muscles to pump water into the rectal chamber. On the "exhale," it squirts the water out.

This arrangement may seem strange, but it brings a side benefit: jet propulsion. When threatened by a predator, a dragonfly nymph folds its legs along its body to achieve a streamlined silhouette, then squirts water out of its anus, hard and fast, for a rocket burst of speed. Nymphs use their jets both for evasive maneuvers and for long-distance travel. A nymph that is ready to emerge must move from the center of the pond to the edge. It may scoot to its destination instead of crawling.

Rectal breathing gives dragonfly nymphs another distinctive talent: They are capable of ballistic defecation, shooting fecal pellets at high speeds over surprisingly long distances. Researchers have measured this phenomenon with some precision in nymphs of the Eastern Pondhawk, which can shoot the pellets about 23 feet. It's not clear what advantage, if any, this unusual skill confers.

Given that dragonfly nymphs breathe through their rectums, you might expect that they end up inhaling polluted water. But nymphs have a way to prevent this potential problem. The nymphal digestive tract packages the fecal matter inside a transparent membrane—a kind of organic garbage bag—before it is launched into watery space. Incidentally, this packaging system makes it easy for scientists to study dragonfly diets. Many prey items can be identified from the indigestible hard parts left behind.

Dragonfly nymphs (and, occasionally, damselfy nymphs) that burrow in sediments rather than clamber around on water plants face another potential pollution problem: They risk sucking in mud as they inhale. The solution is a kind of built-in body snorkel. In nymphs that burrow, the tip of the abdomen is elongated and very narrow; it also bends at an upward angle instead of extending straight out to the rear. So when the nymph burrows into the bottom, its body may be buried, but its snorkel sticks up above the mud into the zone where the water is clear.

Nymph Hunting Strategies

All Odonata nymphs are carnivores, not to mention voracious predators. And they're well equipped for their work. Each nymph has an enormous lower lip, or labium, a hinged, extensible mouthpart that works like an extra arm. The labium has moveable hooks on its leading edge that resemble a pair of sharp-

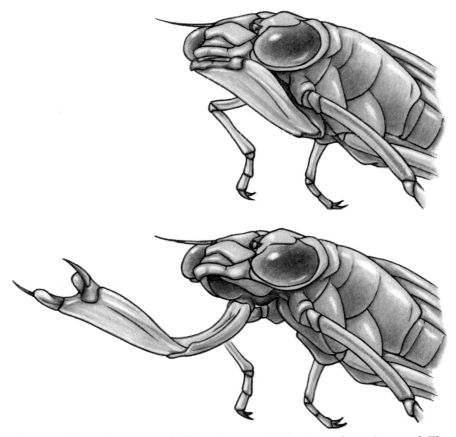

Common Green Darner nymphs like this one can be the top predators in a pond. The nymph's labium, or extensible lower lip, works like a speargun. It's tipped with two sharp hooks and can shoot out at rocket speed to grab a passing tadpole or other prey.

ened pincers. The nymph can unfold the labium in a flash, sending it shooting forward with lightning speed to grab its prey. When the meal is secured, the nymph retracts its weapon to bring the wriggling prey right into its mouth.

In the earliest stages of life, the tiny nymphs take tiny prey, such as single-celled protists, plankton such as daphnia (water fleas) and the shrimplike cyclops, and wormlike nematodes. They learn to avoid prey such as paramecia, single-celled ciliates that are equipped with defensive stingers.

As they grow, nymphs are able to take larger prey such as caddisfly nymphs, mayfly nymphs, stonefly nymphs, mosquito larvae, fish fry, snails, and water beetles. They will also eat other dragonfly nymphs and they can be cannibals, consuming smaller nymphs of the same species.

Scientists describe dragonfly nymphs as opportunistic predators that seize every opportunity to feed—sometimes killing more than they can eat—and take whatever species of prey happens to be plentiful. Virtually any aquatic invertebrate that attracts the nymph's attention and can be subdued and processed into bite-size pieces is fair game. Green Darner and Comet Darner nymphs, which can grow to be 2 inches long, are big enough to hunt down bullfrog tadpoles. In a few taxonomic groups, particularly in some damselfly species, nymphs claim and defend territories, but in most species the nymphs roam their watery environment at will in pursuit of prey.

Dragonfly nymphs use two different hunting styles. One is called "sit-and-wait" or "ambush" predation. Nymphs in the Emerald family exemplify this hunting style. They bury themselves in sediment at the bottom of a streambed and just lie there, motionless, using the sensitive receptors on their extralong legs to detect the vibrations generated by approaching prey. Clubtail nymphs also tend to lie in ambush like this.

Other nymphs are active hunters. Darner nymphs, in particular, often clamber around on submerged plant leaves or across the sandy bottom, stalking prey like a cat after a mouse. Green Darners are also capable of snagging fast-swimming fish fry and tadpoles.

For many dragonfly species, the two hunting styles are not mutually exclusive—nymphs can switch strategies when the situation warrants. Clubtail nymphs, which usually lie buried in sediment till prey blunders by, will switch to active stalking when they are very hungry. Other species may switch from active hunting to ambush hunting to avoid being detected by hungry fish.

Whether they are active hunters or sit-and-wait predators, nymphs detect prey by its movement—either because they see it or because they feel it. Touch-sensitive hunters have small eyes and long antennae. Visual hunters have small antennae and large, well-developed eyes that are capable of discerning shape as well as movement. In one experiment, a nymph avidly pursued a live snail, and then appeared to show equal interest in a dead snail and an empty snail shell—demonstrating that shape, not movement, was what attracted its attention.

Avoiding Predation

Dragonfly nymphs can be the top predators in fish-free environments. But in most aquatic environments—in most ponds, lakes, and rivers—they are both predator and prey. They are food for fish, birds, frogs, turtles, and other aquatic insects, especially giant waterbugs and other dragonfly nymphs.

But nymphs have an array of predator defenses. For one thing, their camouflage colors help them blend into the background. Burrowing nymphs will hunker under a blanket of sand or sediment, and hunters will hide amid dense vegetation, freezing when they sense danger like rabbits do at the sight of a hawk. Nymphs may also use their capacity for jet propulsion to squirt out of harm's way; this is effective for evading salamanders, but not fast-swimming fish. Some nymphs even evade predators by playing dead. Dragonhunter nymphs are known for this behavior. They simply stop swimming and let themselves drift like falling leaves to the bottom of the stream.

If a nymph is captured, it has one last trick in its survival bag: It can shed a leg or, in the case of damselflies, one of its trailing gill plumes, much the way a lizard sheds its tail to get away from a cat. The lost appendage will be replaced during the next molt.

3

Understanding Dragonfly Behavior

Adult, free-flying dragonflies live totally different lives than the water-bound nymphs, with different strategies for finding food, getting around, and avoiding predators. In this stage of the life cycle, they also claim and defend territories and reproduce, spawning future generations of dragonflies that start out as nymphs.

Feeding

Tree Swallows bank and wheel over a pond. Bats flutter around a barnyard at twilight. A flycatcher darts out from a treetop perch. A dragonfly cruises along a row of shrubs. These acrobatic fliers share an unusual ecological niche: They feed themselves by catching insects on the wing.

Dragonflies are the founding members of this elite club, having pioneered the energy-intensive aerial feeding strategy roughly 300 million years ago. Dragonfly expert Jill Silsby, author of *Dragonflies of the World*, calls the dragonfly "the perfect hunting machine."

If you watch closely, you may be able to detect the exact moment when a dragonfly scores a midair meal. Flying purposefully along in a straight-line course, the dragonfly suddenly darts upward or sideways. The capture happens in a blink; to the human eye, it looks like a momentary bobble. Then the dragonfly resumes its steady flight.

Two features that make dragonflies such excellent predators are their sharp compound eyes and their flexible, aerodynamic wings.

Compound Eyes

Dragonflies are unusual among insects in that they rely on a single sense—sight—to detect their prey. They don't need to taste it, touch it, smell it, hear it, or even sense the vibrations it generates in passing—they just have to see it. More than 80 percent of a dragonfly's brain is used for processing visual information. Many insects use their antennae to locate their prey, but dragonflies do not. In one study, dragonflies whose antennae had been removed had no trouble catching prey.

A dragonfly's eyes are very large in relation to its head—indeed, large in relation to the entire body. A typical dragonfly's head is big, round, and shiny, like a motorcycle helmet. Most of the head is made up of the dragonfly's two compound eyes. Other features to note on the head are the face—made up of the frons (forehead), clypeus, and mouthparts—and the ocelli, or simple eyes, which are located at the base of the small bristle-like antennae. The ocelli

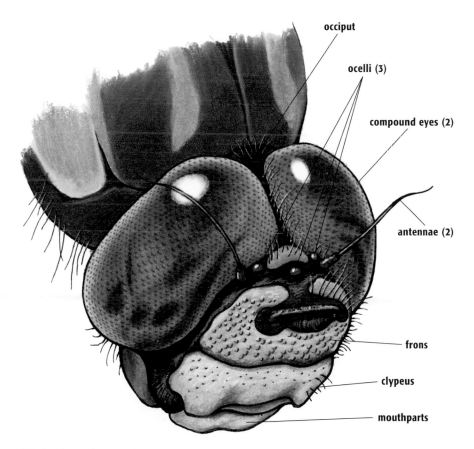

occiput

ocelli (3)

compound eyes (2)

antennae (2)

frons

clypeus

mouthparts

Notice how the two large compound eyes wrap around the head of this Canada Darner. Large, faceted eyes give dragonflies an almost 360-degree view of their surroundings.

aren't capable of resolving images but do detect light; it's thought dragonflies use them to maintain orientation and stability while flying.

The compound eyes are composed of many smaller subunits, called ommatidia, or facets. An adult dragonfly may have ten thousand to almost thirty thousand ommatidia per compound eye.

The big eyes wrap all the way around the head, and each facet faces in a slightly different direction and resolves a separate image. As a result of this arrangement, dragonflies can see in almost every direction simultaneously. The facets that face to the rear do have somewhat lower resolution than the front-facing facets, and a dragonfly's view to the rear is slightly blocked by the wings. But dragonflies can compensate for these impediments with a twist of the head.

Obviously, when it comes to detecting prey, or predators, or mates, having eyes in the back of the head is a significant advantage. But this is not the only visual advantage dragonflies enjoy. Because each eye facet responds independently to stimuli, a dragonfly's eyes are exquisitely sensitive to movement. Fast movements—movements that would be just a blur to human eyes—look sharp and clear to a dragonfly.

Though movement is usually what tips off a dragonfly to the presence of potential prey, some species are also capable of detecting perched and motionless prey by its shape and color. You may see a damselfly, for example, hovering to investigate scars or bumps on a plant stem. The damselfly is interested because the bumps resemble edible insects.

Dragonflies also have excellent color vision. Whereas we humans have a mere three light-sensitive proteins in the retina, allowing us to detect and respond to three colors of light—green, blue, and red—dragonflies can have as many as four or five. In many dragonfly species, one of these proteins is sensitive to ultraviolet light, which human eyes do not detect. Experts think the ability to see in the ultraviolet is especially helpful to dragonflies as they scan the horizon for flying insects—when the prey is backlit against the bright sky. Some species make it a habit to face the sun at twilight, perhaps so that potential prey will be sharply silhouetted. Dragonflies can also see the plane of polarization of light, which the human eye cannot detect; this ability may help them to navigate and to identify bodies of water.

Dragonfly Aeronautics

Dragonflies are such amazing fliers that both the U.S. military and NASA have studied them in hopes of developing aircraft with similar abilities. These insects are powerful, capable of lifting more than twice their own body weight. And they are fast. Their flight can be erratic, so it's hard to get accurate field measurements of airspeed. But according to current best estimates, large, powerful species such as darners are capable of flying at 25 to 35 miles per hour.

Dragonflies are also efficient fliers. Migratory species are capable of covering thousands of miles during their seasonal movements. Even dragonflies that do not migrate may spend most of the day in the air, flying for hours nonstop.

But the main reason that aeronautics engineers admire dragonflies is because they are agile—the most agile of all flying insects. Dragonflies can take off backward, launch vertically like a helicopter, hover motionless for more than a minute, execute an unbanked turn, make a series of dazzling zigzag maneuvers, and stop on a dime.

What makes dragonflies such good fliers? According to Pennsylvania State University researcher Jim Marden, dragonflies have proportionately more body mass dedicated to flight than any other flying creature. A female dragonfly is fully 40 percent flight muscle by weight. Juvenile males start with the same proportion of flight muscle but continue to develop more muscle as they mature. A sexually mature male may be more than 60 percent flight muscle.

Another factor that makes dragonflies good fliers is the design of the wings: lightweight and stiff, yet very flexible. The network of veins acts like the reinforcing struts on an airplane wing. Veins are thickest and strongest along the leading edge, the edge of the wing that cuts through the air. The nodus near the center of the leading edge allows the wing to flex and twist.

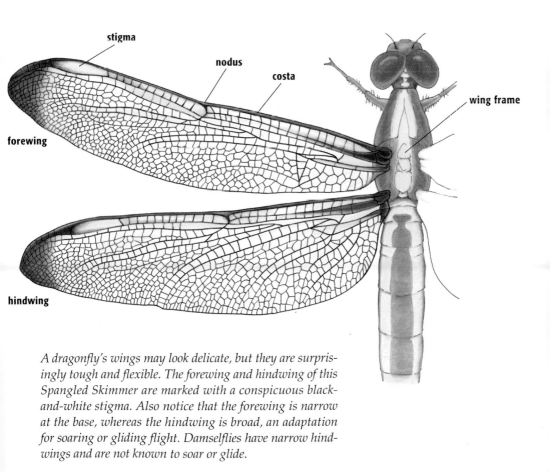

A dragonfly's wings may look delicate, but they are surprisingly tough and flexible. The forewing and hindwing of this Spangled Skimmer are marked with a conspicuous black-and-white stigma. Also notice that the forewing is narrow at the base, whereas the hindwing is broad, an adaptation for soaring or gliding flight. Damselflies have narrow hindwings and are not known to soar or glide.

FLAPPING FLIGHT

A dragonfly's wings beat far too fast for the human eye to see individual wingbeats. If you filmed this high-speed action and then slowed it down, what would you see?

The answer depends on what species you are filming, because dragonflies and damselflies have somewhat different flying styles. A damselfly's wings can generate thrust both on the downbeat and on the upward beat. A dragonfly's wings are jointed in a different way and generate thrust only on the downbeat.

Typically, damselflies beat their wings in a pattern called counterstroking. As one pair of wings strokes downward, the other pair of wings strokes upward, and vice versa. So thrust is generated nonstop by both wings.

Despite the constant thrust, damselflies fly fairly slowly because the air drags on their bodies; they have a comparatively large surface area relative to their very light weight. But even though they're slow, damselflies are still agile. By slanting their wings at different angles, they can juke and jive through the air, evading attackers.

Dragonflies in routine flight use a different wingbeat pattern. Instead of counterstroking, a dragonfly's two pairs of wings usually beat out of phase. The hindwings beat first; then the forewings start their downstroke, lagging one-quarter of a wingbeat behind.

When a dragonfly needs to move very fast—say, to avoid an attacking bird, or to intercept a competing male—it switches to synchronous wingbeats. All four wings flap

When honeybees fly, their two pairs of wings are held together by a zipperlike structure. Dragonflies can move each wing independently, which gives them greater maneuverability. (The clacking sound you hear as a dragonfly turns in midair is the forewing and the hindwing hitting each other during the turn.) This series of images shows a Ruby Meadowhawk on a routine flight. In the topmost image, the forewings are raised, ready for the downbeat.

forcefully downward at the same time, blasting the dragonfly straight up or up and backward. (Some damselflies can pull off this maneuver, too.)

Since a dragonfly's wings generate thrust only on the downstroke, hovering is a challenge—this flight maneuver requires continuous thrust. The dragonfly solution is to fly like a damselfly, by counterstroking: the hindwings beat down as the forewings are lifted, and vice versa. Even though each pair of wings generates thrust only on the downstroke, there are two pairs of wings, so the net result is continuous thrust.

Note that all three types of stroking described so far involve symmetrical flapping, with the right wing and left wing of a pair moving in the same way, at the same time and at the same speed, like two oars on a rowboat. Dragonflies can also execute asymmetrical flapping, with one wing moving independently of the other. This kind of wingbeat is used to execute a fast turn.

To understand how asymmetrical flapping works, think of a canoe traveling downstream, powered by two paddlers. Usually their paddling is symmetrical and synchronous. One person paddles on the right, the other paddles on the left, and the net effect is the same as a single person rowing a rowboat: each stroke is balanced by a simultaneous stroke on the opposite side. The canoe travels in a straight line.

But what if the canoe approaches rapids and sudden turns are necessary to avoid boulders? One paddler can turn the boat with a deft movement of a single paddle—a drawstroke or pry, a sweep or a reverse sweep. Asymmetrical flapping—moving one wing independently of its mate—also lets dragonflies spin on a dime.

The stigmata at the wingtips are thought to act like tiny weights, damping out the vibrations that can develop at high airspeed.

Turbulence is anathema to modern fixed-wing aircraft, but dragonflies both generate and exploit it. The leading edge of each forewing generates a spiral vortex—a mass of spinning air. The rear wings catch this vortex, which enhances lift. The trailing edge of each wing is studded with tiny teeth that force air downward, creating still more swirls of uplifting air. Tiny hairs on the surface of the wings sense airspeed, so the dragonfly can adjust its wing movements to avoid stalling out.

Dragonfly Diet

Adult dragonflies eat only insects—and only live insects at that. Like nymphs, they are opportunistic feeders, and will gobble up whatever happens to be flying around at the moment. If a variety of insects are in the air, dragonflies will eat whatever is most plentiful. It follows that the most common flying insects—members of the order Diptera, the true flies, which includes deerflies, blackflies, horseflies, midges, and mosquitoes—are dragonflies' most common prey. But dragonflies also take large numbers of beetles, flying ants, and other winged insects. They even pursue and eat other dragonflies. In fact, cannibalism is fairly common, although one study suggests odonates eat their fellows only when other prey is in short supply.

A dragonfly typically consumes about 10 to 15 percent of its own weight in prey per day. Given the opportunity, however, some species will eat much more than this. An Eastern Pondhawk, for example, will catch and eat a Blue Dasher that is the same size as itself.

Juvenile dragonflies often eat butterflies and moths, which are common in their forest haunts. They strip off and discard the scaly wings before devouring the bodies headfirst. Dragonflies living in forest habitats also take caterpillars—they may not be flying insects, but as they dangle in midair, suspended on silken threads, they do make suitable targets for aerial hunters.

You may hear it said that dragonflies even eat hummingbirds. This assertion seems to be traceable to a report in the scientific literature of a Common Green Darner grappling with a Ruby-throated Hummingbird. Big dragonflies can be aggressive, and they will attack birds if they feel threatened; the literature also includes a report of a dragonfly in Hawaii attacking a hawk. But it's unlikely that darners make a habit of snacking on hummingbirds.

Catching Prey

Dragonflies have two main strategies for catching insect prey. *Hawking* involves catching insects in flight in midair. This is the most common dragonfly foraging strategy. *Gleaning* involves hovering briefly above vegetation to seize small insects perched on plant stems or leaves.

Birds also use these two foraging strategies, and they most often use their bills to catch prey. Hawking dragonflies frequently catch prey in their mouths; gleaning dragonflies, however, usually use their long legs to pluck up their prey.

Many dragonflies are flexible in their behavior and can switch between hawking and gleaning as needed. Darners and emeralds tend to hawk after food; damselflies are more likely to be gleaners.

When dragonflies are foraging you may see them making systematic patrols across food-rich areas. A dragonfly on patrol will fly back and forth, back and forth, tracing the same path again and again as it looks for food. It may follow a row of bushes, buzz the cattails growing along a lakeshore, or cruise a thicket in the "edge" habitat where a forest abuts a field. There's some evidence that dragonflies remember places that are rich in prey and return to them repeatedly.

Some dragonflies that forage by hawking share a clever strategy with cowbirds and Cattle Egrets. They watch for large animals, such as cattle, horses, or dragonfly enthusiasts wearing oversize rubber knee boots, walking along through tall meadow grass. Then they zip over and follow along behind to catch insects stirred up by the big mammals' passage.

Dragonflies will also hawk after insects that have been attracted to lights at dusk, and they'll even chase the mosquitoes that are attracted to a human's carbon dioxide–rich exhalations—an endearing trait. Though most dragonflies stop flying around sunset, a few species specialize in pursuing the small insects that start to fly in the cool of the evening.

HILLTOPPING

If you take a hike up a local peak in summer, you may find a surprise at the summit: a swarm of dragonflies, far from the nearest open water. This behavior—gathering in swarms in open areas on hills and peaks—is called hilltopping, and some butterflies do it too.

Striped Emeralds and the Mosaic Darners are among the dragonflies that most often engage in hilltopping behavior. A hilltop swarm is not a feeding swarm. Experts think hilltopping is a reproductive behavior—a way to find mates. When a population is small and spread out over a large area, members of the population can have a hard time finding each other. Hilltopping may be a kind of singles scene—it may help dragonflies get together when it's time to mate.

Foraging dragonflies may also be classified as either perchers or fliers. Clubtails, skimmers, and damselflies are among the odonate groups that tend to be perchers. Fliers include the darners, spiketails, cruisers, and emeralds. Perchers claim a tall perch with a good view, such as a grass stem or a dead weed stalk in a meadow, and sit there scanning for prey. If you watch closely, you may see a perched dragonfly cock its head as it follows the air traffic.

Dragonflies typically key in on movement to detect prey, but as they scan, they also note the size and shape of moving objects and seem to calculate whether each item qualifies as prey. No energy is wasted on insects that are too large or too small.

When a perched dragonfly decides that a prey item is both the right size and in range, it makes a sally: It launches from its perch, darts out, grabs its quarry, and quickly returns to its perch. A small insect may be swallowed en route; a large prey item will be carried back to the perch to be dismembered and consumed a bit at a time

Although a sally takes just a few seconds, handling large prey can take many minutes—sometimes as long as half an hour. A perched dragonfly may make just a few sallies per hour, or it may launch from its perch as often as once per minute, depending on the time of day, how many insects are flying, and how big they are.

If perchers behave like flycatchers, fliers are more like Tree Swallows or Chimney Swifts. On days that are good for flying—reasonably warm, with no rain—these dragonflies will be aloft nonstop. They may fly for hours without a break, catching insects on the wing and swallowing them in midair.

Some of the fliers—especially the darners—are known for flying in very large groups called feeding swarms. Sometimes swarms are made up of a single species, all hunting together, but swarms of up to ten different species are also common.

Scientists aren't sure why these feeding swarms form. One idea is that environmental conditions simply force dragonflies into a particular patch of habitat. When it's very windy, for example, dragonflies may gather in sheltered places, out of the wind. It's also possible that feeding swarms form because dragonflies are drawn to a swarm of prey, such as a recent hatch of midges or flies. In shady forests, dragonflies tend to gather in sunny spots, where their insect prey also congregate.

Research on forest birds suggests that members of a mixed-species feeding flock may benefit by hanging out together. They save time and energy because they don't have to bother searching every single nook and cranny—they can watch other flock members to see which places yield food and which do not. Also, the movements of the flock tend to flush insect prey out of hiding, so every individual gets more to eat. And because many eyes are watching for predators, all are safer. It is not known yet whether any of these benefits apply to feeding swarms of dragonflies.

Dragonflies eat flying insects, including damselflies and even other dragonflies. This formidable predator is the appropriately named Dragonhunter. Here it strips off the wings from an Ebony Jewelwing before eating the damselfly headfirst.

Dragonflies in flight catch prey in a couple of different ways. Many dragonflies simply open their mouths and seize small insects with their strong, serrated mouthparts, much the way a flycatcher catches a fly in its beak. Darners, emeralds, and spreadwings are among the dragonflies that typically catch their prey this way.

When tackling larger prey, a dragonfly may use its spiny legs to assist in the catch, or it may use its legs to hang on to the prey while it gets a better grip

DRAGONFLIES AS A PESTICIDE?

Dragonflies eat many insects that humans consider pests, including flies, midges, and mosquitoes. As nymphs, dragonflies feast on water-dwelling mosquito larvae. As adults, dragonflies can eat hundreds of the stinging pests in a single day.

No wonder lots of people have had the bright idea that dragonflies could be used as a form of natural pest control. And at first blush, the idea makes sense. Farmers already use ladybugs and parasitic wasps to control many crop pests. So-called biocontrol is safer than using pesticides. With West Nile virus spreading in North America, why not use dragonflies to get rid of pesky mosquitoes?

There is some precedent for using dragonflies as biocontrol agents. In Asian nations, farmers respect and honor dragonflies because they keep down populations of such rice-paddy pests as stem borers and leaf hoppers. In Australia, dragonfly nymphs helped control cane toad populations by feeding on tadpoles.

Dragonfly nymphs have been used successfully to control disease-bearing mosquitoes exactly once. It happened in the nation of Myanmar in the 1980s. Mosquitoes that carried deadly dengue fever were breeding in the large containers that people used to store their household water. A team of scientists encouraged residents to put a few dragonfly nymphs in each water container. The nymphs went right to work, gobbling up any mosquito larvae that appeared. Public health officials who subsequently evaluated the experiment by measuring adult mosquito populations found them to be acceptably low.

But it's important to note that this experiment in dragonfly biocontrol succeeded because of the conditions under which it was conducted. The nymphs and their prey were living in confined spaces. Nymphs had no choice but to eat the mosquito larvae. They couldn't switch to some other prey when the larvae became rare, the way they would have in the wild.

Though Asian farmers think dragonflies do a good job of controlling pests, it's widely recognized that dragonflies don't wipe out the plant-eating pests altogether. Dragonflies just reduce pest populations to low levels that farmers find acceptable.

In nature, dragonflies—both nymphs and adults—are the ultimate opportunists and eat whatever is plentiful. If mosquitoes are everywhere, dragonflies will eat mosquitoes—and they can definitely make a dent in the mosquito population. But when mosquitoes start to get scarce, dragonflies won't keep searching until they hunt down every last one. Instead, they simply switch to some other insect prey.

So, it may be possible to use dragonflies to control mosquito populations, but not to eradicate them. Ultimately, dragonfly biocontrol is probably impractical as a way to prevent mosquito-borne diseases over a large area.

Dragonflies may groom themselves like fastidious cats—sometimes in the morning before flying, sometimes after copulating or laying eggs. Spurs on the legs work like a comb to remove clingy bits of spiderweb, drops of morning dew, or other foreign matter. Here a Yellow-legged Meadowhawk grooms its antennae (a), the tip of its abdomen (b), and its compound eyes (c).

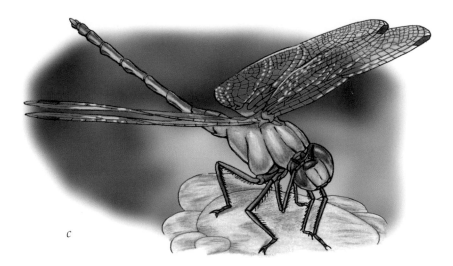

c

with its mouthparts. A bite to the head subdues large insects that struggle. Dragonflies typically discard the wings before eating large prey; if you watch a dragonfly feed, you may see the rejected wings fluttering to the ground below the perch. Dragonflies tend to eat their meals headfirst.

Conventional wisdom has it that many dragonflies also use their legs as a kind of built-in insect net when they feed. The idea is that the dragonfly flies along with its spiny legs held in a cup or basket shape beneath the body, and that this leg basket scoops insects from the air.

Again, there's a parallel for this feeding strategy in the bird world. Most birds in the nightjar family, including the Whip-Poor-Will and the Chuck-Will's-Widow, have a cluster of bristles around the mouth. These birds feed by catching flying insects on the wing, and it's thought that the bristles work like a funnel to increase the chances that an insect will be captured.

The notion that dragonflies carry around their own built-in insect nets is appealing. This purported behavior has been difficult to document, however, and scientists are still investigating whether dragonflies really use their legs this way.

Territoriality

On a warm day in late June, a male Delta-spotted Spiketail cruises along the narrow, spring-fed stream that snakes through a sunny meadow. As the big, green-eyed dragonfly approaches a bend in the stream, a male Twelve-spotted Skimmer launches from his perch on a slender spirea branch overhanging the water. The Twelve-spot barrels straight for the spiketail like a dog after a mail carrier. A collision looks inevitable, but the two dragonflies pull up short. They bob and weave and feint in midair. Finally the spiketail reverses direction and darts away downstream. The Twelve-spot wheels and flaps back to his perch, where he settles down to once again survey the stretch of cold, clear water that is his territory.

A territory, according to the textbook definition, is "a specific area that an animal defends." Territorial behavior is widespread in nature, and has been well studied in birds. Much of what we know about avian territoriality applies equally well to dragonflies.

Most territory holders are males that defend their territories from other males of the same species. In a few species, the females hold territories. And in some species, as in the scenario above, a dragonfly will defend its turf against a member of a different species, and sometimes even against insects that aren't dragonflies. In dragonflies, as in birds, territorial behavior usually begins when the dragonfly is sexually mature; juveniles don't claim territories.

Animals typically claim and defend territories because some valuable resource lies within the territory borders—food, access to mates, or a good place to lay eggs. Defense of a feeding territory is fairly common among birds. Hummingbirds defend patches of nectar-laden flowers, and mockingbirds defend backyard berry bushes. Similarly, a dragonfly may defend a feeding perch—an extra-tall weed stem or a branch that gives a good view over a meadow where insect prey are concentrated. Ebony Jewelwings are one species that defends feeding perches. You may see the same female return to a choice perch again and again over the course of the day. Blue Dashers also defend feeding perches. Both males and females do this, and you may see a good deal of jostling for the prime spots.

In a few dragonfly species, individuals defend not just a perch, but an entire feeding territory—a larger patch of habitat where food is plentiful. Wandering Gliders defend large feeding territories located well away from the ponds where they breed. Defense of feeding territories is not common among dragonflies, however. Usually members of the same species feed together peacefully without aggressive interactions.

Defense of a breeding territory—a place where conditions are ideal for the female to lay eggs—is fairly common but not universal. Species that tend to occur at low densities around the water, such as darners, cruisers, clubtails, and spiketails, usually don't defend breeding territories. There's enough room for everyone. Emeralds, skimmers, and the Broad-winged Damsels—species you'll see around a pond in very large numbers—do tend to claim breeding territories.

In general, males, not females, are the ones that defend breeding territories. One possible reason for this is that by claiming territories, males actually spend less time fighting, and so they save energy.

A typical breeding territory is a patch of sunny, shallow water. (Twelve-spotted Skimmers will abandon an otherwise acceptable territory if it gets shaded over as the day progresses.) Depending on the species, the territory may be chosen because it contains certain water plants or some other substrate that is required for egg laying. Breeding territories can be as small as one square yard or as big as an entire pond. River and stream species such as cruisers and spiketails may claim just a few yards of shoreline or a 50-yard-long expanse.

INVESTIGATING TERRITORIAL BEHAVIOR

If you're curious to see how long your local dragonflies hang on to a territory, how they defend their territories, or how big territories are, you don't need a grant from the National Science Foundation to conduct your own scientific study. By catching a few dragonflies and marking them with distinctive identifying spots, you can keep track of individuals and follow their behavior over the course of time.

To mark dragonflies, you'll need some brightly colored nail polish or white correction fluid. Dab a very small dot of the liquid at the base of one hindwing. To keep track of two dragonflies at once, mark one on the right wing and the other on the left wing, or use different colors.

Scientists have tested this marking technique and concluded that the small dab won't harm the dragonfly or interfere with its ability to fly. A bright color mark may make the dragonfly more conspicuous to predators, but most individuals in a population are eventually consumed by predators. You are not upsetting the balance of nature if you mark one or two dragonflies.

Make sure the mark is dry before you release the dragonfly. Now you'll be able to distinguish this individual from other members of the same species. You can watch to see how long the dragonfly defends a territory; you can track its flight path to determine the size of its territory; and you can observe other behaviors, such as how frequently a perching species leaves its perching post.

Other useful tools for investigating dragonfly behavior are a notebook in which to record your observations; a stopwatch to time the duration of behaviors; and a small thermometer to note how behavior changes as the day warms up or cools down.

In the field, you may notice males exploring along the edge of a pond or stream, looking for the perfect territory. This behavior is especially obvious in male Widow Skimmers. Male dragonflies instinctively know what makes a good breeding territory—this isn't something they have to learn.

Once a male claims a breeding territory, he will either defend it from a perch or fly around it on patrol. The typical size of a breeding territory varies from species to species, and among members of the same species, the territory size also varies with population density. When a population is large, males in that population are more likely to accept smaller territories. They're like dads claiming blanket space on a public beach. If the shorefront is crowded, territories are smaller so that more individuals can fit in the same amount of shoreline.

The number of dragonflies competing for territories can change over the course of the day as well as the season. Early in the morning, dragonflies are waiting to warm up or off feeding. There's not much demand for territories, and an ambitious dragonfly can claim a large patch of real estate. As the morning progresses, however, individuals that have been feeding in outlying areas wing their way to a pond to look for mates. Territories shrink as a result.

The average territory size typically changes with the season in summer species, whose population members keep emerging over an extended period of time. The population is small early in the season but then grows. The average territory size shrinks as the number of individuals competing for space increases.

Finally, territory size is also affected by habitat quality. Territories are larger in poor habitat, smaller in good habitat.

Once a male has claimed a territory, he lets other males know they should stay away. Dragonflies have several strategies for warning off competitors. Some species signal with their brightly colored legs or wings. A colorful face or abdomen can also send a message. Male Common Whitetails fly straight at intruders while holding their bright white abdomens high in the air, like battle pennants. Territory holders also engage in high-speed chases and aerial dog-fights to evict intruders. Any female that would like to slip into an attractive territory to lay her eggs will have to mate with the owner first.

Among birds, a male may defend a breeding territory for weeks to months. Male dragonflies, in contrast, typically defend their breeding territories for just a few minutes to a few hours. Ebony Jewelwings are thought to hang on to a territorial perch for as long as a week. And sometimes a territory holder may disappear for a while, then show up again. Perhaps the tired male took time off to feed or rest, or perhaps he was at another pond, defending a different territory.

Holding a territory is hard work. It takes time and energy to drive competitors away, and constant patrols make the territory holder conspicuous and vulnerable to predators. There's also the risk of being injured in a territorial dispute with other males. But a male dragonfly with a good territory is likely to have a much better reproductive output over his lifetime, and after all, that's what the game of life is all about—leaving behind as many offspring as possible and perpetuating your personal gene pool.

Reproduction

Courtship

A bunch of flowers, a nice dinner, a flirtatious glance—these behaviors are part of what we understand as human courtship. Scientists use the term courtship to mean any set of predictable behaviors that occur before intercourse. Different species have different courtship rituals; groups of closely related species often have similar ones. Courtship may involve a gift of food, distinctive vocalizations or other sounds, or some kind of dancelike performance or display of strength or aggression by the male.

Courtship behavior may seem romantic, but it has several very practical purposes. At the most basic level, it helps the individual establish that a prospective mate is a member of the same species. Beyond that, the male's courtship display often helps a female make up her mind about her choice of mate. Often the courtship ritual sends a signal that the male is genetically fit and would make a good mate.

Courtship behavior is very common in nature, especially among birds, fish, and insects, and it has been particularly well studied in birds. Among the odonates, courtship behavior is common in damselflies, but it is uncommon in dragonflies.

Courtship rituals among jewelwings—members of the genus *Calopteryx* in the Broad-winged Damselfly family—are easy to observe in the field. Typically a female enters a male's territory and settles on a perch. Then the show begins, as the male flies toward her, hovers, and postures to show off his most colorful feature. Depending on the species, he may adopt a pose that gives a good look at his face, legs, wings, or even the underside of the abdomen. In this case, the male turns around and does the damselfly equivalent of "mooning" his female visitor. If the female is unimpressed with the show, she simply flies away. But if she finds his display acceptable, she stays put on her perch.

Eastern Amberwings, members of the Skimmer family, are one of the few North American dragonfly species to perform an elaborate courtship ritual. The male amberwing spends a lot of time scouting for the perfect patch of water plants—just right for egg laying. When he finds a good location, he claims a territory and waits. If he spots an approaching female, he hustles out to meet her, then escorts her through his domain, leading her to the optimal egg-laying site. He hovers over his little patch of open water, showing off his fine accommodations.

When a female dragonfly says no to an advance, she curves her abdomen downward. Although females sometimes turn down their suitors, male damselflies and dragonflies don't suffer rejection nearly as often as male birds and butterflies do.

Most dragonfly species dispense with the niceties of courtship, however. Females typically spend most of their adult life away from the water, foraging in a forest or field. They approach the water only when they are ready to lay their eggs. Among those species where the males don't hold territories, a male dragonfly simply intercepts a female as she approaches the water. Among those species that do hold territories, the owner grabs whatever female enters his domain.

Males tend to outnumber females around the water, as the females hang around in the forest till the last minute, so you are likely to see some ferocious aerial fights as several males compete for one female. Sometimes the males make mistakes in their frenzy, and several males wind up hooked together in a chain, with the lone female at the end.

Self-insemination

Dragonfly sex involves one very unusual step: Before a male can mate with a female, he first must mate with himself. Self-insemination doesn't happen in any other insect group, although the procedure is fairly common among spiders.

A dragonfly's abdomen is made up of ten segments, and the male genitalia—including the sperm-producing apparatus—are located in segment 9, near the tip of the abdomen. But male dragonflies also have accessory genitalia, located on segments 2 and 3, near the base of the abdomen. These include a sperm storage reservoir and a penis (see page 54).

Before he can mate with a female, the male dragonfly has to move sperm from the tip of his abdomen into the storage reservoir at the base of his abdomen. The female dragonfly is inseminated when her genitalia make contact with the male's accessory genitalia, *not* with the genitalia at the tip of his abdomen.

To make the sperm transfer, a male dragonfly typically settles on a perch and curls his abdomen beneath his body, so that his genitalia on segment 9 touch the accessory genitalia on segments 2 and 3.

Exactly when this self-insemination step takes place differs for damselflies versus dragonflies. Male dragonflies make the sperm transfer while they are alone, just before they hook up with a female. Male damselflies, in contrast, latch on to a female first, then quickly make the sperm transfer before mating with the female.

Tandem Flight

Before dragonflies can mate, the male and female must literally hook up in what is called the tandem position. It's quite common to see damselflies or dragonflies hooked together in tandem flight. The dragonfly in the lead is the male; he is using claspers at the tip of his abdomen to tow the female behind him, like a truck with a trailer.

Sometimes a tandem pair will touch down in pondside shrubbery, giving you a chance to take a careful look at just how they are stuck together. Damselflies and dragonflies hold on to their mates in slightly different ways. A male damselfly has four claspers at the tip of the abdomen that grip the female at the top edge of her thorax. The claspers fit into a plate on the female's thorax in a kind of "lock-and-key" mechanism. A male dragonfly has only three abdominal claspers—one on the bottom and two on top—that grip the female by the back of her head. Sometimes a dragonfly male grips his mate so hard that he scratches and damages her eyes.

It's a common misconception that dragonflies flying around in tandem are mating. In fact, they are not. Either they are getting ready to mate, or they have already mated and the female is laying her eggs. When the male is towing the female around, her genitalia, which are located at the tip of her abdomen, are nowhere near either of the male's two sets of genitalia. Before mating can actually occur—before the female can receive sperm from the male—the tandem pair has to adjust their body positions and move into a configuration called a copulation wheel.

Mating

The copulation wheel is unique to dragonflies among all other insects. Achieving the position takes several steps. First, the pair must take up the tandem position, the male gripping the female's head or thorax with his claspers. Next, the female reaches up and grabs the male around the tip of his

A male Comet Darner claims a female, but before the two can actually mate, they must first link up in the tandem position. Hooking up is a three-step process: The female perches and the male lands on her back; the male curves his abdomen under his body and grabs the female around her eyeballs with his claspers; and the pair flies off with the male in the lead.

abdomen with her six legs. Then she does a deep body bend, folding her abdomen up underneath her thorax. (Imagine hanging by your arms from a chin-up bar with your body perfectly straight, then jackknifing at the waist to bring your legs up, parallel to the floor. That's roughly the maneuver.) This move is what makes it anatomically possible for the two dragonflies to mate. Finally, the female presses the tip of her abdomen against the male's accessory organ.

A female Yellow-legged Meadowhawk (bottom) curves her abdomen around to receive sperm from her mate. At the moment of contact, the two dragonfly bodies form a heart shape. The unromantic scientific term for this pose is copulation wheel.

Romantic souls are pleased to note that at the climactic moment, the two slender bodies form a delicate heart shape. Experts say the pair is now "in cop."

Damselflies like to find a secluded perch, safe from predators, where they can form their copulation wheel—in thick bushes or high in the treetops. Dragonflies are more likely to form the copulation wheel while flying. In this situation, the male may do the flying for both, or he may hoist his abdomen a little higher in the air so the female can get her wings into a horizontal position and help with the flapping.

In some species, the process of transferring sperm from male to female can happen very quickly—in as little as three seconds. In other species, it can take as long as an hour. And often, before he discharges his own sperm, the male spends some time in another activity, sperm displacement.

A female dragonfly can mate repeatedly, and in the mating frenzies that happen over a pond, she often does. As a result, when a male grabs a female, she may already have sperm inside her body, left over from a previous mating. Even if she has already laid some eggs, she may not have used up her stored sperm supply. This sperm remains viable and could be used to fertilize more eggs.

So the male dragonfly takes a step that will help make sure *his* genes are passed to the next generation. He uses his spoon-shaped penis either to scoop out or tamp down the old sperm before he adds his own. Most of the time that two dragonflies are together in a copulation wheel, they are not actually mating. Instead, the male is occupied with evicting or compressing the sperm deposited by a previous male. When this job is done, he desposits his own sperm fairly quickly.

Egg Laying

Female dragonflies are ready to lay their eggs immediately after mating. Another name for egg laying is ovipositing, from the Latin *ova*, meaning egg, and *ponere*, meaning to place.

In some dragonfly species, the female has a sharp abdominal appendage called an ovipositor, a bladelike tool she uses to cut little slits in the stems or leaves of water plants. Then she pushes the eggs safely inside. If you look very closely at the stems of water plants, you may see the neat little patterns left by ovipositors. Usually eggs are inserted below the waterline, but in some species, the female anticipates rising water levels and oviposits above the waterline. Females of other species place their eggs in moss, rotten wood, tree branches, or damp soil or mud rather than in water plants. Damselflies and darners are among the groups that have true bladelike ovipositors.

Female clubtails, cruisers, emeralds, and skimmers lack a bladelike ovipositor and mostly drop their eggs in the water, usually by tapping the water with the tip of their abdomen while flying. In some species, however, the female simply jettisons the eggs as she flies along. Sometimes, the male helps with this process, flying along in tandem with the female and swinging her around like a golf club to shake the eggs out. A few skimmer females have a

a

b

Dragonflies lay eggs in several different ways. a) A female Eastern Pondhawk simply scatters her eggs on the surface of the water. b) Female baskettails (this one is a Prince Baskettail) lay a sticky string of eggs, which they attach by one end to clumps of water plants. c) Damselflies and darners like this female Swamp Darner use a sharp ovipositor to neatly insert eggs inside plant stems or leaves. d) This female Twin-spotted Spiketail plunges her ovipositor into the bed of a shallow forest stream, leaving eggs safely hidden in the soft sediments.

c

d

slightly different strategy: They dip their abdominal tips in the water and, like a golfer making a chip shot, splash egg-laden droplets up onto water plants or shoreline mud.

Female baskettails are egg droppers with an unusual strategy. They perch on shoreline plants to methodically extrude a long string of eggs around 6 inches long. This string coalesces in a sticky ball at the tip of the female's abdomen. Then the female flies with her egg ball out over the water. She finds a suitable underwater plant and dips her abdomen to release the ball; one end sticks to the plant, while the string unfurls into the water.

Still other species drop their eggs on floating debris, wet moss, or tangles of water plants. A few species even drop their eggs on dry grass that is due to be flooded in spring.

Spiketails are a special case. Females have ovipositors, but not very elaborate ones. A female spiketail uses her ovipositor to lay eggs in mud or sediment rather than plant tissue. The process is fascinating to watch. The female hovers upright over very shallow water, then drives her body downward, abdomen-first, to plunge the ovipositor into soft mud or stream sediments. Pumping up and down in a constant rhythm, she looks like an oversize sewing machine needle.

Pictures of several different ovipositors can be found on page 54.

Guarding

Once two dragonflies have mated, that may be the end of the relationship. In some species, the female goes quietly to the water to lay her eggs, placing them in secluded, sheltered places—under a streambank or in a thick stand of pond plants. Meanwhile, the male wings off to look for another mate.

In other species, however, the male protects his paternity by standing guard over the egg-laying female. If another male should swoop in, seize the female, and mate with her *before* she can lay her eggs, it's the second male's sperm that will fertilize the eggs.

Male dragonflies who guard their egg-laying mates may stand sentry in one of two ways. In contact guarding, the male continues to fly in tandem with the female while she lays her eggs. In noncontact guarding, the male stays nearby while the female lays her eggs but does not actually touch her; he may either perch near his mate, usually on pond plants, or hover in the air above her as she lays her eggs. In either case, if other males come by and show interest in his mate, he chases them away.

Contact guarding is a very common behavior among pond damselflies and spreadwing damselflies. You'll also notice this behavior in some dragonflies as well. In particular, certain skimmers—those species that do not defend territories—engage in contact guarding.

Some darners, such as the Common Green Darner, also engage in contact guarding. A pair of these large, colorful dragonflies flying around in tandem is an amazing sight. The male protects his mate from assaults by other males as she touches down here and there to insert her eggs into water plants.

Unescorted female dragonflies are assaulted by eager males, so this male Common Green Darner (in front) hangs on to his mate while she tucks some eggs inside the stem of a water plant. The behavior is called contact guarding.

Green Darners in tandem make stately progress around the pond. Damselflies that lay eggs in tandem move even more slowly, in a kind of bumbling progression. In contrast, a pair of skimmers laying eggs in tandem moves very fast, since the female doesn't have to stop and cut slits in plant stems. She just dips her abdomen to drop eggs in water or wet mud.

In some species of contact-guarding damselflies, the female ducks right underwater to lay her eggs, inserting them into a leaf or stem that is below the waterline. In some species, the male hangs on tight and ducks under, too. In other species, the male lets go before he gets a bath. He may latch back on to his mate when she emerges.

Only the skimmers that do not defend territories protect their mates by contact guarding. Skimmers that defend territories are satisfied with noncontact guarding. This makes sense: The male is guarding his territory, and the female is laying her eggs within his territory, so she's protected in that way. Many jewelwing damselflies are territorial, and these species also are noncontact guarders.

A male's guarding behavior may be flexible and change depending on the situation. He may guard his mate jealously when she first starts to lay eggs but relax his attention as she gets close to finishing her work.

Each style of mate guarding has its pros and cons. A contact-guarding male who hangs on to his mate can be absolutely sure that she has not mated with another male—all of the eggs his partner lays will produce offspring with his genetic contribution. On the other hand, males who do not contact guard can significantly increase their reproductive output if they take a little initiative. At the same time a male Common Whitetail is standing guard near an egg-laying female, he often manages to sneak in a second mating with another female. Then he just stands guard over the two females at once.

Temperature Regulation

Insects, spiders, fish, amphibians, and reptiles are among the animal groups referred to as cold-blooded, because their bodies take on the temperature of the environment. That's in contrast to warm-blooded animals, such as mammals and birds, which maintain their bodies at a constant temperature through internal metabolic processes.

Cold-blooded animals do have a variety of ways to adjust their body temperature. Often it's as simple as adjusting the body position. On cold mornings in spring or fall, you're likely to see dragonflies basking like lizards in the sun. It's not simple pleasure that causes them to seek the sun's warmth. A dragonfly's flight muscles must be warm before it can fly. This can be a matter of life and death. If the muscles are not warm and the dragonfly can't fly, it can't avoid predators, and it can't find food or mates.

Dragonflies select flat surfaces in full sun as basking sites. Early in the morning, when the sun is low and rays of sunlight penetrate the atmosphere almost horizontally, a vertical surface such as a stone wall or tree trunk makes a good basking site. If it's still cold at midday, when the sun is directly overhead, dragonflies will bask on a horizontal surface such as a wide, flat rock or a fallen log that receives the sun's direct rays. Dragonflies in cool, shady forest habitats tend to adjust their positions relative to the sun all day long, like suburban tanning enthusiasts dragging their lounge chairs around a tree-shaded backyard.

Although different species of dragonflies prefer different perching positions—darners tend to perch vertically, for example, and clubtails horizontally—these preferences may go out the window if a dragonfly really needs to warm up. It will adopt whatever position gives maximum exposure to the sun. Occasionally dragonflies even find heat sources other than the sun; there's one report of Yellow-legged Meadowhawks "basking" on a warm compost pile.

Besides basking, dragonflies have other ways to keep warm. On a cool, windy day, you may see a Blue Dasher perched with its wings drooping rather than out to the sides in the usual position. Held close to the body, the wings act like a windbreak, reducing heat loss through convection.

A change in position can help a dragonfly cool off as well as keep warm. At the height of summer, at midday, some dragonflies seek shaded perches.

This is a familiar pondside sight—a Common Whitetail spread-eagled on bare ground or flat rocks, basking in the sun. Dragonflies often bask in the morning to warm up their flight muscles before lifting off.

Some species have dark or dark-spotted wings that they can use like parasols to create shade for their bodies. Dragonflies that spend the day in full sun in open meadows may obelisk to minimize the amount of sunlight striking the body. An obelisking dragonfly looks like it's doing a headstand, with its head down and abdomen raised. In this position, the dragonfly's body receives less of the sun's rays when the sun is directly overhead, in the same way that you are exposed to less sun when you are standing up than when you're lying on your stomach on the beach.

Obelisking behavior is not very common among dragonflies. Only about thirty of the more than three hundred North American species are known to obelisk. They include members of the Broad-winged Damselfly family, Club-tail family, and Skimmer family. Blue Dasher, Calico Pennant, Halloween Pennant, and Eastern Amberwing are some of the species you're most likely to see obelisking.

If you stand and watch an obelisking dragonfly for a while, you may notice that it fine-tunes its position as the sun moves across the sky, keeping its abdomen at the proper elevation and pointed in the right direction to minimize sun exposure. Not every dragonfly found standing on its head is obelisking, however. In territorial males, a raised abdomen can be a threat posture. And if the sun is low in the sky, a dragonfly doing a headstand may actually be trying to warm up, not cool off. Early and late in the day, the sun's rays strike almost horizontally, so a headstand at this time of day exposes *more* of the body to the sun's warming rays.

When you get overheated at the beach, you go for a dip. Dragonflies do this too. You may see one zip out over the water, drop down to hit the surface with a splash, then quickly fly up with a little shivery shake. For some reason, dragonflies tend to triple-dip, splashing three times in quick succession. Dipping is an effective way to cool off, and it also may be the way dragonflies drink to replace fluids lost in hot weather.

All dragonflies can adjust their internal temperatures by adjusting their behavior. A few species—the largest dragonflies, the most powerful fliers—are also capable of generating their own body heat to some extent. Instead of relying on the sun to warm up their muscles, these dragonflies are like athletes who stretch out before running. They warm up their muscles through a process called wing-whirring.

You may see this behavior in an adult dragonfly on cold mornings: The dragonfly vibrates its wings very fast while perched. It looks as if the dragonfly is shivering, which in a sense it is. The rapid muscular contractions generate heat. Wing-whirring behavior is also common among teneral dragonflies, because they typically emerge just before dawn, when—even at midsummer—the air can be cool. Common Green Darners on migration may start wing-whirring before sunrise to ensure an early departure. Male dragonflies that need to defend territories or females that are busy laying eggs may wing-whir to warm up as the day cools down. Many species of dragonflies have a

An obelisk is a pillar of stone. Perched on a cloverhead, this Blue Dasher is obelisking—imitating a narrow column as it points its abdomen skyward. The behavior helps dragonflies stay cool when the sun is overhead, because light strikes only the tip of the abdomen, not the entire body.

layer of what looks like hair or fur on the thorax. Like real fur, the fuzz helps hold in the heat generated by those muscle contractions.

Dragonflies that fly for hours nonstop also generate a lot of heat with all that flapping. But as the day wears on and the air heats up, they face a new thermoregulatory challenge: They need to vent the excess heat so they don't cook themselves. Dragonflies solve this problem by increasing the rate at which body fluids circulate. As a result, heat is carried away from the hairy, insulated thorax and out to the long, slender, hairless abdomen. Like a desert jackrabbit's long ears, the abdomen has a comparatively large surface area, so heat is radiated efficiently out into the atmosphere.

A few dragonfly species, notably the Common Green Darner, can regulate their temperature by changing color. They do this thanks to heat-sensitive pigments in their skin. When it's hot, refractive granules that scatter light become concentrated at the surface of the skin. If the air cools down, dark granules migrate to the surface of the skin, replacing the reflective granules. The dark pigments absorb the sun's heat and help the dragonfly warm up. Most dragonfly species that have these changeable pigments look bright blue when it's hot and change to dark purple or gray when it's cold.

Preying on Dragonflies

Even though dragonflies are fierce and fast, agile fliers, they are not immune to danger. Predators and parasites take a toll on their populations.

Predators

Among the predators that regularly catch dragonflies are some of the world's fastest birds. In North America, two falcon species—the American Kestrel and the Merlin—fuel their fall migration flights by preying on the Common Green Darners that migrate south along the same routes. The Sharp-shinned Hawk is another raptor species that takes dragonflies during fall migration. In the spring, when newly emerged dragonflies are plentiful, raptors catch large numbers of the tender tenerals to feed their downy chicks.

Other fast-flying birds that take dragonflies on the wing include nighthawks, swifts, flycatchers, Purple Martins, and various swallows. Ducks and herons don't usually pursue flying dragonflies, but they do gobble up the just-emerged tenerals resting on pondside vegetation. Bats are another winged predator, but not an important one, since most dragonflies stop flying around the time bats start flying at dusk.

Other dangers lurk around the margins of a pond. A female dragonfly that lays her eggs unguarded by a male is especially vulnerable to an ambush by a frog or fish when she pauses at the water's surface. Unwieldy dragonfly pairs laying eggs in tandem also may be easy prey. Besides frogs and fish, some of the larger pond insects, such as back swimmers and giant water bugs, also seize dragonflies that hesitate at the water's surface. A few species of wasp specialize in taking dragonflies; the female wasps lay their eggs on the dragonfly corpses, which become food for the wasp larvae after they hatch. The smallest dragonflies and damselflies sometimes get snagged in spiderwebs, though with their keen vision, odonates usually avoid these traps.

Dragonflies also have to watch out for carnivorous plants. Sundew plants (*Drosera* species) are especially common in bogs. Nutrients are in short supply in bog habitat, and sundews are among the plants that have adapted to the situation by nourishing themselves with insect prey. Their spoon-shaped leaves are edged with spikes that ooze a sticky liquid. A damselfly or small dragonfly that recklessly alights on a sundew may get trapped in the goo. Then a leaf curls around its body, and the sticky liquid starts the process of digestion.

Foiling Predators

Most sexually mature dragonflies are brightly colored and conspicuous, but a few species continue to rely on camouflage at this life stage. For example, Gray Petaltails have mottled gray bodies that blend perfectly with the tree trunks they favor as perch sites.

A few conspicuously colored skimmers seem to use mimicry as defense against predators. Female Eastern Amberwings, for example, look a lot like venomous wasps. And when a dragonfly curls its abdomen up over its back, it looks strikingly like a scorpion. When a clubtail adopts this pose, the bulge at the tip of the abdomen looks like the head of a snake that is rearing back to strike. This scary sight may fool birds that are gleaning fast through foliage and don't get a really good look at the "snake."

In addition to fast flight and deceptive colors, dragonflies have a few other tricks for foiling predators. If a damselfly is perched on a twig and spots a predator nearby, it may sidle around the circumference of the perch, like a squirrel circling a tree trunk, keeping the twig between its body and the source of danger. Female Ebony Jewelwings, which have a habit of clapping their wings while they are perched, will freeze like rabbits if they spot a predator nearby. Dragonflies may even play dead, falling to the ground, where they lie still, awkwardly sprawled and apparently lifeless, until the danger passes. Some of the pond damselflies—the bluets and forktails—are particularly prone to this deception. If caught, dragonflies will fight back. They can bite with their sharp mandibles and stab with the sharp tips of their abdomens.

Parasites

In addition to predators, dragonflies are often plagued by parasites. Several water mite species spend part of their life cycle as parasites on adult dragonflies. Large enough to be seen with the naked eye, these mites look like small orange or red dots clustered on the dragonfly's thorax or abdomen or along the wing veins.

Parasitic mites have a curious life cycle. Adult females lay their eggs in water. As soon as the tiny mite larvae hatch out, they start looking for a host— a dragonfly nymph that is ready to emerge. The mites latch on to the nymph and ride along as it crawls up out of the water. When the new teneral dragonfly struggles out of its old shell, the mites have to hustle. They clamber off the old exoskeleton and reattach themselves on their now-winged host.

The mites' piercing mouthparts penetrate the new dragonfly's skin and cement themselves in place. For the next few weeks, the mite larvae ride around on the adult dragonfly, sucking its body fluids as it flies and feeds. Finally, when the time is right and the dragonfly is flying low over the water, the mites bail out and jump back into the water. There they undergo another transformation, to become water-dwelling nymphs. And once back in the water, they stop being parasites and adopt a predatory lifestyle before maturing to adulthood and completing their life cycle.

If a very large number of mites attach themselves to a single dragonfly, they can kill it outright by sucking it almost dry. Usually, though, the mites just kill the dragonfly's chances of contributing its genes to future generations. A male dragonfly infested with a hundred or more mites is often too weak to battle with other males and claim a mate.

Mites are the most common dragonfly parasite, but you also may spot small parasitic midges on the wings of such migratory dragonflies as the Common Green Darner. The midges look like small, dark smudges on the clear wings. Like mosquitoes, the females of this parasitic species need a blood meal to nourish their eggs. They will feed for a few days and then detach.

Migration

Ecologists define migration as "seasonal movements made by an entire population of animals." Typically a migrating population is moving *away* from difficult conditions, such as drought or food shortage, and *toward* a place where conditions are more favorable for feeding or breeding.

The seasonal migrations made by many birds are a phenomenon familiar to most people. Many North American birds fly south in autumn, spend the winter resting and feeding in subtropical or tropical habitats, then fly north again in spring to the places where they breed. But birds are hardly the only animals that migrate. Caribou make seasonal treks across the arctic tundra between their breeding and feeding grounds; wildebeests and zebras migrate across the plains of Africa; and great whales migrate across entire ocean basins. Monarch butterflies take several generations to complete their annual migration cycle.

Migration is not a common behavior among dragonflies, but it happens. Of the more than three hundred dragonfly species found in North America, about sixteen species from just two families, the darners and the skimmers, are known to be migratory. Migratory species featured in this book include the Common Green Darner (the species you are most likely to see migrating), Twelve-spotted Skimmer, Blue Dasher, Wandering Glider, Spot-winged Glider, and Black Saddlebags. In Great Britain, the Wandering Glider is known as the Globe Skimmer, for the way it travels the globe.

Dragonfly migrations aren't as conspicuous or as well studied as the migrations of birds, fish, and large mammals. For one thing, dragonflies usu-

MASTER MIGRATOR:
THE COMMON GREEN DARNER

In Ontario, Canada, you may see Common Green Darners flying as early as April—even though the ice is barely off the ponds, even though it is far too cold for any Green Darner nymphs to have emerged from the gelid local waters. Indeed, drag a net across the bottom of the pond and you'll find Green Darner nymphs aplenty—nymphs that are not quite big enough to be ready to emerge.

So where did those early-flying dragonflies come from? As with Canada Geese, it seems that there are at least two distinct populations of Common Green Darners in North America—residents and migrants. The dragonflies that are still nymphs in April, swimming around underwater, are residents. The early ones that are flying around in the chilly air are migrants.

Resident Common Green Darners have a life cycle that's simple to understand. New adults emerge in summer—typically late June in northern latitudes. Over the course of the next month, these free-flying adult dragonflies forage, fatten, find mates, and breed. The female dragonflies lay their eggs in late July, and the eggs hatch as soon as they are laid. Then eleven full months go by as the nymphs feed and grow underwater. It will be late June of the following year before a new generation of adults emerges.

Migrant Common Green Darners follow a different, more compressed schedule. The ones that arrive in Ontario in April emerged from warmer waters somewhere to the south; exactly where is not clear. If conditions permit, they will breed soon after they arrive in the northlands in early spring. The nymphs will hatch out right away, and they will develop much more quickly than the nymphs of the resident population. After just a few months, as autumn arrives, a new generation of migrants is ready to emerge. Prompted by instinct, these new adults start winging their way south.

Scientists still aren't sure exactly where these migratory dragonflies spend the winter. It's possible the entire migratory population travels all the way to a single ice-free locale such as Florida. But it's also possible that subsets of the migratory population are touching down at a variety of intermediate locations along the migration route. Or individuals may breed repeatedly while flying south, leaving a chain of offspring in ponds from Maine to Florida. More study is needed to solve these migration mysteries.

ally ride air currents very high in the sky, out of sight of most human eyes. Also, dragonfly migrations don't seem to happen with the same clockwork regularity as bird migrations, though certain species do make predictable, steady movements southward in the fall and northward in the spring. Finally, dragonflies don't always make their migrations in large groups. When they're migrating alone or in small groups, it's hard to distinguish their movements from those of the resident species.

But dragonfly migrations can be big and dramatic, involving entire swarms rather than just a few individuals. In autumn of 1992 a migrating swarm of more than a million Common Green Darners moved along the shore of Lake Michigan, passing through Chicago's lakefront. Migration swarms are more likely to form in fall than in spring.

In the fall, dragonfly migration may start as early as late July and continue into mid-October. September is the peak month. Swarms tend to follow large landscape features such as lakeshores, mountain ridges, and coastlines. If it's a good day to watch migrating hawks, it's also a good day for migrating dragonflies—the movements of both groups are strongly influenced by the weather. Look for mass movements just after a southbound cold front passes through the area. Like raptors, dragonflies depend on thermals—rising currents of warm air—to loft them high in the air, up to the altitude where steady winds will speed them on their journey south.

Migratory dragonflies, like migratory birds, tend to have long wings relative to their body size. This is an adaptation for sustained flight. Also like birds, migratory dragonflies have the metabolic ability to pack on a store of fat before traveling. A typical Common Green Darner in midsummer will be about 22 percent fat by dry weight, but specimens taken at Cape May, New Jersey, during one fall migration were nearly 30 percent fat.

Dragonfly migration is an instinctive behavior. Individuals don't have to learn the route from their parents or peers—they just know the way. The dragonflies that make up migrating swarms are often juveniles, only recently emerged and not yet sexually mature. For the most part, the wind carries them to their destination, but it's thought that dragonflies navigate by following linear landforms such as streambeds and shorelines, and possibly by using the sun as a compass.

4

Species Identification

Field Marks

This chapter includes a field guide to the most common and widely distributed dragonflies in eastern North America. Most of them can be identified at a distance by field marks—distinctive characteristics that may include colors, patterns, shape, or size of various parts of their bodies. Field marks may be found on any of the body sections—head, thorax, or abdomen—as well as on the wings and other appendages.

Many dragonflies have brightly colored faces and eyes. These colors can be distinctive field marks, so take a good look at the dragonfly's head.

On the thorax, an important field mark in many species is a set of contrasting shoulder stripes or side stripes. The color of the legs and their thickness, length, or degree of spinyness can also be clues to a dragonfly's identity.

Most dragonflies have transparent wings, but they may be dark-colored or spotted, banded, or mottled. So wing color and pattern can also be field marks. The patterns formed by the wing veins and the size and color of the stigma can all be clues to a dragonfly's identity as well. In fact, dragonfly taxonomists use the pattern of veins in the wings as a key tool in classifying species, although a detailed discussion of wing venation is beyond the scope of this book.

Like the thorax, the abdomen is often brightly colored and may be marked with a pattern of spots, bands, or stripes. These colors and markings are all useful field marks. Female dragonflies tend to have fatter, wider abdomens than males of the same species.

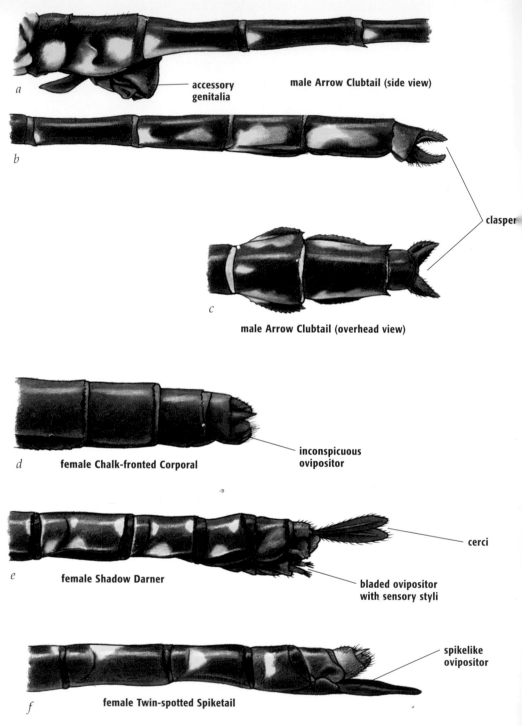

a accessory genitalia — male Arrow Clubtail (side view)

b

c male Arrow Clubtail (overhead view)

clasper

d **female Chalk-fronted Corporal** — inconspicuous ovipositor

e **female Shadow Darner** — cerci — bladed ovipositor with sensory styli

f **female Twin-spotted Spiketail** — spikelike ovipositor

The size and shape of abdominal appendages can be a clue to a dragonfly's sex. Males have accessory genitalia at the base of the abdomen (a) and claspers the tip (b, c). The female's ovipositor may be barely visible (d), small (e), or large (f).

Both male and female dragonflies may have conspicuous abdominal appendages. The size and shape of these appendages can also be field marks. Males typically have set of distinctive claspers at the very tip of the abdomen, used to hold on to the female during mating. A male's accessory genitalia look like a big bump on the underside of abdominal segments 2 and 3. Some female dragonflies have a conspicuous ovipositor at the tip of the abdomen. Also, some females have a pair of abdominal appendages called cerci. In most species, the cerci are small and pointy, but in a few species, they are large and leafy and can serve as a field mark.

Making an ID

To identify a dragonfly in the field, follow these seven simple steps.

1. Study Your Field Guide

Leaf through the pictures in the field guide section to familiarize yourself with the species you're most likely to see. This field guide includes the 27 most common and widespread species in the eastern half of North America. Admittedly, that's a small subset of the approximately 125 damselfly species and more than 300 dragonfly species known to occur in North America. But if you visit a typical small pond on a midsummer day, you should be able to spot most of the 27 species featured here.

You'll probably see some species not listed in this book as well. And you'll definitely see species not listed in this book if you go dragonfly-watching in habitats other than ponds. To identify the less common species, you'll need another guide, such as those listed in the Resources section.

2. Determine Whether You Are Looking at a Dragonfly or a Damselfly

When you spot your quarry in the field, first ask yourself if you are looking at a dragonfly or a damselfly. One clue is the overall size. Damselflies tend to be small, slender, and dainty-looking. Dragonflies tend to be bigger and more robust.

Most often, you can tell a dragonfly from a damselfly by the way the insect holds its wings when perched. If the wings are pressed together, up over the back, it's probably a damselfly. If the wings lie flat, straight out to the sides, it's likely a dragonfly. The exceptions to this rule are spreadwing damselflies, which hold their wings flat, not folded up over their backs. But you can tell a spreadwing is not a dragonfly because the wings are not perpendicular to the body; they are slanted at an angle.

If you're still not sure whether you've got a damselfly or a dragonfly, here's another distinguishing feature to check for: Are all four wings the same shape? Then it's a damselfly. Or are the hindwings wider than the forewings? If so, it's a dragonfly.

Also take a look at how the eyes are positioned on the head. A damselfly's eyes are set far apart. Try to imagine placing a third eye in between them; with a damselfly, there would still be room left over. A dragonfly's eyes are set closer together—so close that there would not be room for a third eye placed between them. In some dragonfly families, the eyes are set so close together that they actually touch one another.

If you observe the insect flying, how would you describe the flight? Damselflies look weak in flight and tend to flutter. They also tend to stay low, usually just above the surface of the water or close to pondside vegetation. Dragonflies tend to be powerful, fast fliers. You are more likely to see them cruising around at high speeds, out in the open.

3. Determine the Family Group

The next step in identification is to decide what family the specimen belongs to. The two Odonata suborders of dragonflies and damselflies are made up of about twenty-five smaller groups called families. Each family is made up of groups of related genera (the plural of genus). Each genus contains a number of closely related species. The species featured in the field guide section come from three different damselfly families—the Broad-winged, Spreadwing, and Pond Damselflies—and from six different dragonfly families—the Darners, Clubtails, Spiketails, Cruisers, Emeralds, and Skimmers. What follows is a brief look at some of the characteristic traits that distinguish each of these families.

DAMSELFLY FAMILIES

The Broad-winged Family. These damselflies have wider wings than other damselflies, as their name indicates. And whereas most damselflies have transparent wings, broadwings have quite colorful wings—indeed, at a distance you might mistake a broadwing for a butterfly. Broadwings are medium-size damselflies, and many species have iridescent bodies in shades of green, blue, or red. They also have conspicuously long, spindly legs. You see broadwings in flight around streams and rivers.

The Spreadwing Family. These damselflies get their name from their habit of perching with their wings spread partly open rather than folded up over the back. Spreadwings may be small or medium-size, and they have clear wings. Most members of this family have metallic green or bronze bodies and blue faces; male spreadwings often have blue eyes as well. They can be found in a number of different habitats—around ponds and marshes as well as temporary pools. They seem to prefer places where water plants grow very thickly.

The Pond Damsel Family. Pond damsels often live around ponds, although you'll also find them in lake, bog, and stream habitats. They are the most common damselflies, abundant and easy to spot. Small to medium-size, they have clear wings and short legs, and they're known for their comic-strip colors: They come in turquoise, kelly green, lipstick red, tropical orange, bright yellow, and even purple.

DRAGONFLY FAMILIES

The Darner Family. Darners get their name from "darning needle," a common folk name for dragonflies, although insect darners are far larger than the heavy-duty sewing needles housewives once used to repair worn stockings. At the very tip of the abdomen, female darners have knife-like blades attached to their ovipositor. It's used to jab holes in water plants so the female can lay eggs inside.

The Clubtail Family. These dragonflies are easy to recognize by their club-shaped abdomens—slender at the base, but bulging at the tip, like a baseball bat. Some members of this family are comparatively small, but the group also includes the massive Dragonhunter, which is bigger than a Ruby-throated Hummingbird. Most clubtails sport military camouflage colors—yellow or green stripes on a black or brown background. You see clubtails along shaded streams and rivers.

The Spiketail Family. Like darners, these dragonflies are often quite large. They get their name from the female's spike-shaped ovipositor. Spiketails tend to be mostly black or brown; like clubtails, they are striped, but whereas clubtails have all-over camouflage stripes, spiketails tend to have just two or three distinct, light-colored stripes on the thorax. Many species have blue or green eyes. When it's time to lay eggs, the female spiketail hovers in a vertical position over a shallow forest stream and bobs up and down, up and down, like the needle on a sewing machine. As she bobs, she pokes her spike into streambed mud or sediment, leaving her eggs in a safe hiding place.

The Cruiser Family. These dragonflies are fast fliers, and males "cruise" for long distances along streams, rivers, and lakes in their search for prey or for mates. These long-legged, medium to large dragonflies can be distinguished by the single pale stripe on each side of the thorax, by the yellow stripes on the face, and by the pattern of spots on the abdomen.

The Emerald Family. Emerald dragonflies have luminous green eyes and, like the jewel they are named for, they're rather rare. Probably that's because many species breed in uncommon habitats, such as sphagnum bogs. Some members of this group have iridescent green or bronze-green bodies as well as green eyes, but most have plain brown bodies. The males of some emerald species have distinctive spindle-shaped abdomens, wide at the middle and narrow at the ends.

The Skimmer Family. These dragonflies prefer to skim above the still waters of ponds and marshes, not fast-flowing rivers and streams. Because they're big and common, they are some of the easiest-to-see dragonflies. As a group, skimmers are strikingly diverse and are represented by a large number of species. In North America there are slightly more than three hundred dragonfly species from seven dragonfly families; about one-third of these species are skimmers. Skimmers come in a rainbow of colors, and many species also have conspicuous patterns on their wings. To add to the impression that skimmers exist in bewildering variety, females often look strikingly different from males of the same species.

4. Take Note of the Habitat

Bird-watchers know that habitat can be a clue to identity. For example, there are many species of sandpipers, and they all look much alike. Most prefer beach habitat, but a few species live in open meadows. So if you see a sandpiper in a meadow, you can be sure it's not one of the beach species.

Habitat can also be a clue to the identity of dragonflies. The rare Gray Petaltail, the only member of the Petaltail family found in North America, lives around natural springs that seep out of wooded hillsides, and nowhere else. So if it's in the wrong habitat, even if it looks like a Gray Petaltail, it's probably not.

Many species of dragonflies are aptly named. Meadowhawks like to perch in meadows; pondhawks patrol around ponds; river cruisers are found along streams and rivers; and the beaverpond baskettail really does hang out around beaverponds.

Also think about the season and whether you are likely to find this species in this habitat at this time of year. For example, most species of the speckled streamside dragonflies called Mosaic Darners emerge in summer; only a few emerge in spring. So if you see what looks like a Mosaic Darner flying along a stream in early spring, you know it's not one of the summer species.

5. Watch How the Dragonfly Behaves

Several aspects of a dragonfly's behavior can be important clues to its identity, including its perching style and its feeding, mating, and egg-laying habits.

Perching style. Some dragonfly species are perchers and others are fliers. Perchers spend most of their time sitting on perches and make only brief, low flights. Fliers fly high and fast, often nearly nonstop.

Also notice *where* the dragonfly perches. Does it touch down in trees? At the tips of weed stems? On flat rocks by the water? Is it low to the ground or high in the treetops?

The position a dragonfly takes when it perches can be another clue to its identity. It may perch vertically, with its head up, tail down, and body parallel to the perch; horizontally, with the body parallel to the ground, perhaps sit-

Facing page: *The Calico Pennant (a) tees up at the tips of weed stems. The Harlequin Darner (b) perches in a vertical position, with its body parallel to an upright perching post. The Widow Skimmer (c) often perches in an oblique position, with its body at an angle to an upright support. Damselflies and clubtails, including this Cobra Clubtail (d) most often choose a horizontal perching position on a leaf, a flat rock, a log, or even right on the ground.*

a

b

c

d

ting on a flat leaf or rock; at an oblique angle to its perch site; hanging, with its body suspended vertically from an overhead twig or stem; or "teed up," with its body held horizontal at the tip of a weed or branch.

Feeding habits. Keep an eye on the dragonfly in flight to see if you can determine what type of prey it's taking, or train your binoculars on the dragonfly's mouth when it returns to its perch with prey. Clubtails tend to take large prey; darners and spiketails tend to take medium-size prey; and many cruisers, emeralds, and skimmers take tiny prey known as "aerial plankton." Most dragonflies fly solo when foraging, but a few species are known for their habit of gathering in large "feeding swarms."

Mating and egg-laying habits. Watch for behaviors related to reproduction. If the dragonfly is a male, does he appear to be defending a territory? Is he making regular patrolling flights, coursing up and back over a patch of open water? Is he chasing other males away when they come too close? Do you see a pair flying in tandem or forming a copulation wheel? Some species routinely mate while airborne; others typically settle on a perch.

If you spot a female, does she appear to be laying eggs? Is a male flying in tandem with her while she lays or guarding her by hovering or perching nearby? Or is he nowhere to be seen? Different egg-laying behaviors are characteristic of different species. Notice whether the female is dipping her abdomen in the water, plunging it into mud or sediment, or sawing into plant stems with her ovipositor.

6. Make Careful Note of Any Field Marks

Size. Size can be a diagnostic trait. For example, most darners are big, and most skimmers are medium-size, although a few are tiny. Illustrations in a field guide are not always lifesize; a dragonfly that looks large in a tight close-up may be rather small in real life. In this field guide, a size icon shows you the dragonfly's approximate size (see page 63).

Also take note of the relative sizes of different parts of the body. Is the abdomen long or short relative to the wings? Is it slender or wide? Are the legs comparatively long or short? (Some damselflies and some clubtails are characterized by extra-long legs.) Do the wings seem wide or narrow? (Wandering Gliders are known for their very long wings, which are useful on long migration flights.)

Shape. Shape can also be diagnostic. A club-shaped abdomen is characteristic of clubtails and some cruisers as well. A spindle-shaped abdomen is characteristic of emeralds.

Color. What color or colors are the eyes and face? What color is the thorax? The abdomen? Does either or both have noticeable stripes or spots? A dragonfly's body color changes as it ages, from freshly emerged teneral to juvenile to sexually mature adult. In many species, mature adults develop an opaque, waxy coating called pruinescence; this coating looks like a layer of powdered chalk—white, pale blue, pink, or purple—dusted over the body. What color are the wings? Are they clear, spotted, or colored? Also check the stigma color. Overall, do the field marks you see match one of the illustrations in the guide?

Sex. In some dragonfly species, males and females look almost exactly alike. In other species, they appear quite different. Often the males are more brightly colored—and hence easier to identify in the field—than the females. Some field guides include pictures of both males and females; in other guides, only the male is shown. In this field guide, the female is pictured if she looks significantly different from the male.

If your guide shows mostly males, and if you spot a dragonfly that doesn't match any of the pictures in your guide, consider that it may be a female. Watch closely to see whether this unidentified dragonfly is hanging around with an easy-to-identify male. Is the mystery dragonfly laying eggs? Is there a male guarding nearby? If your mystery dragonfly hooks up in tandem with a known male, that's good evidence they're the same species. Dragonflies do occasionally hook up with a member of the wrong species, but this is pretty rare.

If no mate is in evidence, try to determine the sex of the unknown dragonfly. Females usually have thicker abdomens than males of the same species. Viewed from above, the female's abdomen tends to be the same width along its entire length; the male's abdomen, in contrast, is often narrower at the base or the tip.

Another way to determine a dragonfly's sex is by the number and shape of the abdominal appendages. Male damselflies have a set of four claspers at the tip of the abdomen, whereas male dragonflies have three claspers. Females typically have just two terminal appendages, the cerci. Also, only males have a visible bump at the base of the abdomen, under segment 2, where the accessory genitalia are located. And only females, though only those of certain species, have a visible bump on the underside of segment 8 or 9, where the egg-laying structures are located.

Also take a look at the wings. In many dragonfly species, the shape differs for males versus females, with the males' hindwings having a "cut-out" area at the base, and the females' hindwings smoothly rounded. You can't use this trait to determine sex in skimmers and Green Darners, however; in these groups, males' and females' wings look alike.

7. Refer to the Species Accounts

Compare the field marks and behavior with the illustrations and information in the species accounts. Make the ID.

DRAGONFLY TIMELINE

This dragonfly calendar shows which species you are most likely to see as the dragonfly season progresses from spring through summer to fall. Species listed as being especially common in one season may also be present in other seasons, but in smaller numbers. Individuals also may emerge at different times in different geographic locations. How fast a nymph develops is influenced by the water temperature and by how much food is available. A species that has a wide geographic distribution will emerge earlier in the milder southern states, than in colder northern states.

Early Spring

Common Green Darner

Spring

Springtime Darner

Common Baskettail

Lancet Clubtail

Emerald Spreadwing

Eastern Forktail

Common Whitetail

Early Summer

Familiar Bluet

Ebony Jewelwing

Twin-spotted Spiketail

Black-shouldered Spinyleg

Illinois River Cruiser

Slaty Skimmer

Prince Baskettail

Midsummer

Widow Skimmer

Twelve-spotted Skimmer

Blue Dasher

Eastern Pondhawk

Calico Pennant

Halloween Pennant

Fawn Darner

Late Summer/Early Fall

Wandering Glider*

Spot-winged Glider*

Black Saddlebags*

Shadow Darner

Late Fall

Yellow-legged Meadowhawk

All Season Long

Common Green Darner

*These species fly year-round in deep southern latitudes. In northern latitudes they are among the earliest immigrants but are especially conspicuous in early fall.

Species Accounts

The species presented here are organized into family groups. Each species is identified by two names: a common name and a scientific name. What this book calls "common names" are more precisely referred to as "English-language dragonfly names used by many Odonata enthusiasts in North America." Why this distinction? By convention, a common name is a name that ordinary people, not scientists, made up long ago, a name that people have been using spontaneously for quite some time—perhaps decades or centuries. Thus, the names used here can't really be considered common names, because they are not folk names handed down through generations. These names were assigned to North American dragonflies only recently, by a committee of scientists from the Dragonfly Society of the Americas. Before the committee made up these English-language names, most dragonflies in North America didn't have conventional common names. After all, most people don't pay much attention to dragonflies. To the average person, a dragonfly is just a dragonfly, and never mind what species.

Although most dragonflies have historically lacked common names, there has been a long tradition of assigning them scientific names. In the two-part scientific names given here, the first word is the genus, and the second is the species. It's conventional to capitalize the genus name, lowercase the species name, and italicize both genus and species.

A genus is a group of closely related species within a family. The genus *Libellula*, for example, is a large one that includes *Libellula luctuosa*, the Widow Skimmer; *Libellula lydia*, the Common Whitetail; *Libellula pulchella*, the Twelve-spotted Skimmer; *Libellula incesta*, the Slaty Skimmer; and many others. The genus *Libellula* is in the Skimmer family, a large family made up of many other different genera (the plural of genus), including *Celithemis*, the Pennants; *Sympetrum*, the Meadowhawks; *Pachydiplax*, the Blue Dashers; and *Pantala*, the Gliders, just to name a few.

Note on size icons: Each of the species in this section includes a silhouette set to the size of an average specimen:

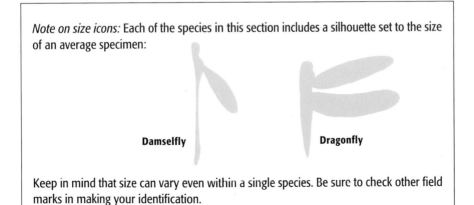

Damselfly

Dragonfly

Keep in mind that size can vary even within a single species. Be sure to check other field marks in making your identification.

Ebony Jewelwing *(Calopteryx maculata)*
Broad-winged Damselfly Family (Calopterygidae)

MALE

About the name: This damselfly's distinctive matte black wings have earned it its name. The genus name *Calopteryx* means "beautiful wing," and indeed, many members of this genus have boldly patterned or iridescent wings. The species name, *maculata,* is Latin for "spotted" and probably refers to the prominent white spots at the tips of the females' wings.

Description: Large for a damselfly, with a body that's about 2 inches long and a wingspan of about 2½ inches. Males can be identified by their dark-colored wings and their iridescent, blue-green bodies. The wings are unusually wide, which makes the narrow abdomen appear even more slender. The legs are another distinguishing feature, jet black and very long. Females look like faded males. They have brownish wings and dull bronze bodies. Each wing is tipped with a conspicuous white stigma. Males lack this feature.

Habitat: Ebony Jewelwings sometimes show up at small ponds, but usually you'll find them along slow-moving, shallow woodland streams.

When you'll see them: From spring to summer.

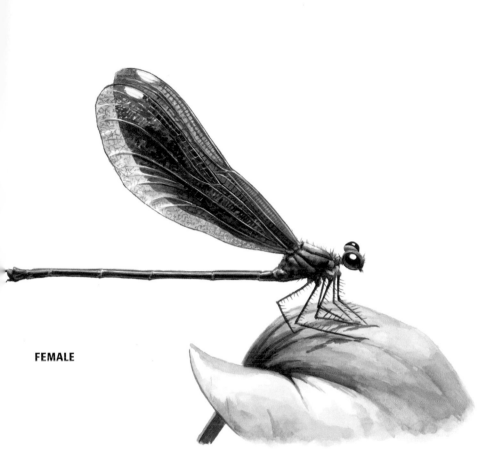

FEMALE

Behavior: Ebony Jewelwings are perchers, known for their habit of sitting for hours on streamside vegetation. Sitting still probably helps these damsels avoid predators, such as larger dragonflies, that cue in on movement. From their perches on plants at the water's edge, Ebony Jewelwings make short flights out over the water to capture gnats and other small insects. Their flight is often described as slow and bouncing.

When they perch in between flights, both males and females sometimes clap their wings. Wing clapping is thought to be one way that mates communicate—sort of like hand signals. But there's also evidence that wing clapping helps jewelwings cool off by increasing blood circulation to the extremities. This behavior may also improve the intake of oxygen.

Each male defends a small territory and will chase other males away from it. The male also does a fluttering courtship display when females are around. After a pair mates, the female lays her eggs in his territory, either on floating or submerged water plants. The male remains nearby, guarding her even as he tries to woo other females.

Similar species: The female Smoky Rubyspot looks similar, with dark wings and a green to dark brown abdomen. The male Smoky Rubyspot has a dark abdomen.

Emerald Spreadwing *(Lestes dryas)*
Spread-winged Damselfly Family (Lestidae)

About the name: Most damselflies fold their wings up over the back when they perch, parallel to their long, narrow body. Spreadwings get their name from their habit of holding their short wings open when they perch, with the wings at an angle to the body. A male Emerald Spreadwing is distinguished by the iridescent emerald green sheen all over his upper body surfaces. The genus name *Lestes* is Greek for "robber" or "pirate"; most likely this name was chosen because the Emerald Spreadwing dashes out from its perch to grab prey, a behavior that reminded some observers of a stealthy robber. The species name *dryas* is Latin for "wood nymph."

Description: This is a medium-size damselfly; the body is about 1 1/2 inches long. The transparent wings are very short in proportion to the body. Males have azure eyes and a gorgeous, glittering metallic green sheen on the upper thorax and abdomen. Sharply contrasting with the glittery green are the pale, powder blue surfaces on the underside of the thorax and the tip of the abdomen. Females are bronze-colored overall.

Habitat: As nymphs, Emerald Spreadwings are very active hunters, but their bold activity puts them at risk of being eaten by fish. As a consequence, Emerald Spreadwings are most common in habitats that lack fish: small, shady woodland ponds and shallow marshes that dry up in summer. The nymphs also tolerate alkaline water.

When you'll see them: Adult Emerald Spreadwings emerge in late spring and early summer. Some populations lay their eggs in ephemeral spring pools that will dry up in late summer and fall. In this case, the eggs enter a state of suspended animation after they are laid, so that the nymphs do not hatch out until the next year, when spring rains refill the pools.

Behavior: Like most damselflies, Emerald Spreadwings are perchers and make only short flights. Usually you'll spot them clinging to emergent water plants. Males do not hold territories. Instead, they actively search for the females, which feed in open areas away from the water. Males that fail in their quest head back to the pond and hang around, waiting for a chance to intercept and mate with a female who has been brought there by a more successful male. Mated pairs fly in tandem while the female inserts her eggs into the stalks of emergent water plants. She leaves the eggs above the waterline.

Similar species: Closely related species such as the Swamp Spreadwing and Elegant Spreadwing are similar in appearance but larger, with duller colors.

Familiar Bluet *(Enallagma civile)*
Pond Damselfly Family (Coenagrionidae)

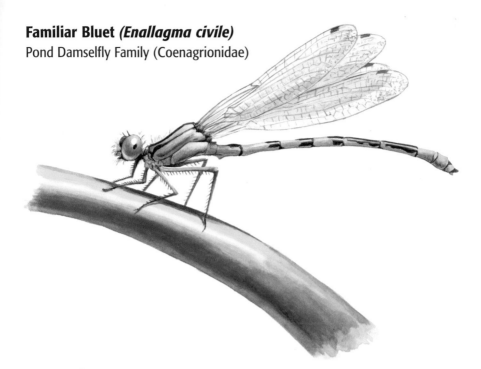

About the name: The family name Coenagrionidae includes the Greek root word *agrio* or "fields," imply-ing a wild creature living in the fields. Bluets are a large group within the Coenagrionidae, and they get their name from the turquoise color characteristic of many males in this group. *Enallagma* comes from the Greek *enallax*, meaning "alternate," plus *agma*, "a splinter"; it's thought that this name refers to the alternating black and blue stripes on the abdomen. The species name *civile* is Latin for "the masses," an allusion to how com-mon and abundant this species is.

Description: This is a medium-size damselfly, about 1½ inches long. You'll notice male bluets from a dis-tance because of their striking color. Up close, the male has a blue thorax with black stripes and a blue abdomen banded with black rings. The eyes are black with blue eyespots. Wings are transparent. Females look like bleached-out males, except the abdomen has a central black stripe instead of rings.

Habitat: This is the archetypal "pond dragonfly." It's ubiquitous around permanent and temporary ponds, but you can also find it near slow-flowing streams and often around ornamental backyard pools. Familiar Bluets are colonizers and spread quickly into new habitats. Once they were considered a denizen of southern states exclusively, but they have been spreading northward for the past century.

When you'll see them: Summer.

Behavior: Like most damselflies, Familiar Bluets are perchers—weak fliers that don't go far from cover. They like to perch low, often on the ground or on logs or low-growing plants. Bluets often gather in breeding aggregations, so you may see a whole group of bluets all busily laying eggs in the same patch of water plants. Bluets may form these groups for one of the same reasons that birds form flocks and fish swim in schools: pro-tection from predators. Though damselflies are known for their courtship displays, in this species mating begins without ceremony. Then the pair flies in tandem, touching down to test for submerged water plants where the female can place her eggs. When she finds the right place, the female submerges, abdomen first. By doing so, she is able to insert her eggs into plant tissue that is well below the surface; this ensures that the eggs will be protected from drying if the water level drops. As for her mate, he starts to sink with her but usually lets go before his head gets wet.

Similar species: At least thirty-five bluet species exist in North America, and the males, with their charac-teristic blue-and-black (or yellow, orange, or red) bodies, are very hard to tell apart in the field. The amount of black on the abdomen and the size and shape of eyespots can be clues to identity, but close inspection of the shape of the male claspers is usually needed to make a definitive identification.

Eastern Forktail *(Ischnura verticalis)*
Pond Damselfly Family (Coenagrionidae)

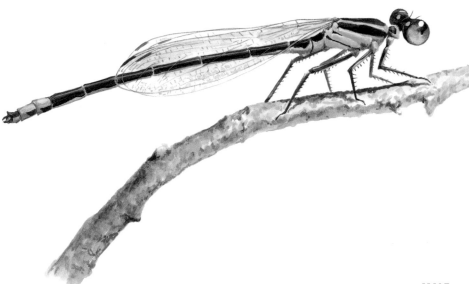

MALE

About the name: We call them forktails in North America, a name that's a nod to the tiny but distinctive forked structure at the tip of the male's abdomen. In Great Britain, they are called the Blue-tailed Damselflies because so many species have a conspicuous blue spot at the tip of the abdomen, sometimes referred to as a "taillight." This is the Eastern Forktail because it's the most common forktail in the East, and there's a western counterpart, the Western Forktail, *Ischnura perparva*; the two species' ranges overlap in the prairie states. The genus name *Ischnura* comes from the Greek *ischnos*, meaning "withered, thin, or weak," plus the Greek *uro*, meaning "tail"; members of this group do have especially thin and delicate-looking abdomens.

Description: These are very small damselflies, about 1 inch long, with a wingspan of 1¼ inches. They are so small and light, a strong wind can carry them away. As a consequence, this species spreads easily and quickly into new habitats. Males have a bright electric green thorax marked with wide black stripes. The abdomen is dark with a pale blue tip. When this damselfly is in flight, the dark abdomen blends into the background, so that all you see is the green thorax and blue abdominal tip. This can result in an optical illusion: Your eyes interpret the scene as a small blue bug persistently chasing a bigger, bright green bug.

Females pose an identification challenge because they change color as they age. Typically, immature females have an orange thorax with black stripes, a mostly black abdomen, and black eyes with orange eyespots. Mature females develop an all-over gray-blue, powdery coating.

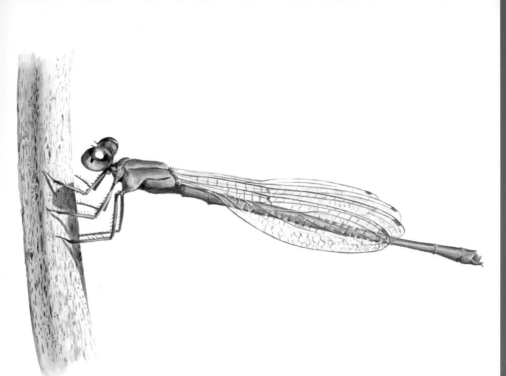

FEMALE

Habitat: These damselflies are happy in a variety of habitats, but they favor still water—small ponds and slow-moving streams with plenty of aquatic vegetation. You may also see them along woodland trails, feeding or resting in the sun.

When you'll see them: Eastern Forktails are some of the first damselflies to emerge, showing up around ponds very early in spring. They have a long flight season, with new individuals continuing to emerge from the water through early fall.

Behavior: Eastern Forktails are classic perchers and rarely buzz out over open water, preferring to linger among the shoreline weeds. You're most likely to spot Eastern Forktails while they are perched horizontally, low to the ground, on branches or plant stems or on the ground itself.

The submerged water plants on which females lay their eggs provide good habitat for the nymphs that hatch out. Once the tenerals emerge, they develop very quickly into sexually mature adults; females have been seen laying eggs just four days after emerging. Females sometimes carry out a threat display to warn off intruders, curling the abdomen downward while rapidly beating their wings. They are also unusual among damselflies for their habit of mating just once; most damselflies take a series of partners.

Similar species: In locations where their ranges overlap, it's easy to confuse male Eastern and Western Forktails.

Common Green Darner *(Anax junius)*
Darner Family (Aeshnidae)

About the name: Members of this family are called hawkers in Great Britain and Australia, in homage to their skill at catching insects in midair. Here in North America, we call them darners, perhaps for their sewing-needle shape, perhaps for the superstitious—and entirely false—belief that, given the opportunity, they will sew your eyes or mouth shut. Voracious hunters, Common Green Darners are one of the few species that had a common name—in fact, a few common names—before the Dragonfly Society of America scientists officially assigned them one; many people know them as Mosquito Hawks. As for the scientific name, *Anax* is Greek for "lord" or "king," and these powerful predators seem to be everywhere in June, hence *Anax junius*, "Lord of June."

Description: These are very large dragonflies—close to 3 inches long. You'll be impressed when you see them! Male Common Green Darners sport a bold color pattern: grass green on the entire upper body—eyes, face, and thorax—with a contrasting, bright blue abdomen accented by a dark brown stripe up the center. The eyes meet on the top of the head along a visible seam, a characteristic darner trait. Also look for the distinctive bull's-eye mark on the forehead—it looks like a miniature archery target. The wings are clear.

Females, like males, are green on the thorax but may be any color from gray to dull red on the abdomen.

Habitat: Common Green Darners prefer still-water habitats such as ponds, marshes, and pools, especially when these places are crowded with water plants; their nymphs like to clamber around in the underwater thickets. They do accept a wide variety of habitats, however. After heavy summer rains, you may see them gather at temporary wetlands to lay their eggs. Females often feed in open fields, meadows, and upland clearings, far from the nearest source of water.

When you'll see them: This is one of the first dragonfly species to start flying in early spring and one of the last species still flying around in fall. Some populations are resident—living in the same location year-round—but others are migratory. In fall, you may see migrants gathering in large swarms to wing their way south.

Behavior: During the long summer days, adult Common Green Darners seem to fly nonstop from dawn to dusk, rarely stopping to perch. If you do spot a perched darner, it's probably a juvenile, and it's likely to be hanging vertically from a grass stem or sturdy weed.

As nymphs, Common Green Darners prowl through submerged vegetation, actively stalking their prey. Adult males cruise through the air at high speeds with flickering wingbeats, patrolling up and back in their shoreline territories. These big dragonflies prey on a variety of insects, including other dragonflies, and they often join the dragonfly feeding swarms that form late in summer. Of all the darners, this is the only species where the male engages in contact guarding. He holds on to the female as they fly in tandem, and she lays her eggs in floating water plants or rotting logs. Her sharp ovipositor slices into the soft material so she can leave her eggs inside.

Similar species: The Male Eastern Pondhawk also has a green thorax and blue abdomen, but it is much smaller than the Common Green Darner.

Shadow Darner *(Aeshna umbrosa)*
Darner Family (Aeshnidae)

About the name: Dragonflies in the genus *Aeshna* are called Mosaic Darners because their dark abdomens are decorated with an intricate pattern of blue, green, or turquoise spots; the overall composition resembles a tiled mosaic. The genus name *Aeshna* is Greek for "ugly" or "misshapen," which seems like a strange choice for such lovely dragonflies. As it turns out, there's evidence that the entomologist who named them in the eighteenth century intended to bestow upon this genus the name *Aechma*, from the Greek for "spear." Through a printer's error, however, that name was transformed into *Aeshna*. The species name *umbrosa* means "shady," a reference to the Shadow Darner's preferred haunts, and also to its habit of flying late in the day, when the light is fading.

Description: This is a large darner, about 2³/₄ inches long. The wings are about 1³/₄ inches long. Both male and female Shadow Darners are dark brown overall, with a rusty brown thorax and a dark brown abdomen. The eyes are brown to blue-green, set in a pale blue-green face. Two greenish-yellow stripes on each side of the thorax are easy to see in the field. Males have small, pale blue spots marking the top of the abdomen; females may have green or blue spots, or a combination of the two colors. Females also have a noticeably thicker abdomen than males, with two very obvious abdominal appendages (the males have three appendages). The wings are clear.

Habitat: Shadow Darners like it shady. They're found around woodland beaver ponds, bogs, and shaded, slow-moving streams; they also fly at the edges of forested areas and along forest roads.

When you'll see them: Shadow Darners may appear in spring, but they are most numerous from mid-summer through fall and may even linger till first frost.

Behavior: Typical fliers, Shadow Darners sometimes remain active until after dark. When they do stop to perch, they tend to hang vertically from twigs high in the treetops. Male Shadow Darners will claim a small portion of a stream where they patrol regularly, staying in the shade near the streambank and about a foot or so above the water. As a shade-loving species, these darners tend to be most active in the late afternoon and evening. They sometimes join feeding swarms. Females lay their eggs in wet, decaying wood.

Similar species: The Mosaic Darners are a fairly large group of closely related dragonflies, all with very similar field marks, including bold stripes on the thorax and a mottled abdomen.

Springtime Darner *(Basiaeschna janata)*
Darner Family (Aeshnidae)

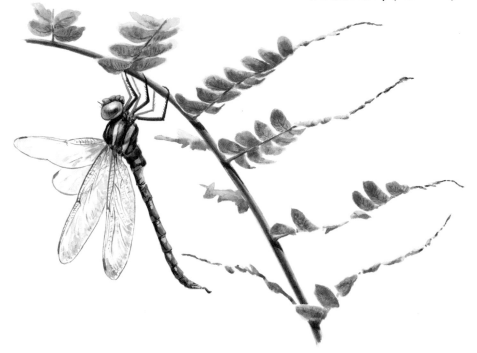

About the name: Springtime Darner is the perfect name for this species because it emerges very early in spring, before most of its relatives. The prefix *basi* in the genus name indicates that experts consider this a "primitive" species (think "basic" or "baseline"); it is less evolutionarily advanced than some of its relatives. The species name *janata* may be a reference to Janus, the Roman god for whom January is named. The connection is that this dragonfly starts to fly very early in the year.

Description: This is another large, brown, streamside dragonfly, about 2¹/₂ inches long. Male and female Springtime Darners are quite similar in appearance. Two bold, slanting, cream-colored stripes on the brown thorax are a distinctive field mark. Sometimes these stripes shade to green on the upper ends. The abdomen is brown and marked with light blue spots, sometimes green in females. The wings are clear, with small brown spots at the base, although the spots are hard to see in the field. The eyes are a dull gray-blue.

Habitat: These dragonflies favor slow-flowing woodland streams and rivers and well-oxygenated ponds and lakes—places where aquatic plants don't grow too thickly.

When you'll see them: The flight season of Springtime Darners is long, starting in early spring and continuing into midsummer or even early fall in warm climates.

Behavior: Springtime Darners perch either vertically or in the oblique position. Most often they choose a perch site that's low to the ground, although sometimes they can be spotted hanging high in trees.

Check the jumbled piles of sticks and debris that accumulate at a stream's edge to see the slender, green-and-brown nymphs. As adults, Springtime Darners do not join feeding swarms the way other darners do. They are most active around midday but are sometimes still flying at sunset. The males move in an erratic course that takes them out over shallow water. This is one of the few dragonfly species that keeps on flying even when it rains.

Females lay their eggs in water plants. You may see a female land on a floating leaf, then back up until she is positioned at the edge of the leaf, with her abdomen hanging down below the waterline. Then she uses her sharp ovipositor to puncture the plant and insert her eggs.

Similar species: The Springtime Darner resembles a smallish Shadow Darner, but these two species fly at different times—Springtime Darners early in spring, Shadow Darners later in summer. See also the notes on Fawn Darner.

Fawn Darner *(Boyeria vinosa)*
Darner Family (Aeshnidae)

About the name: Young deer, called fawns, are brown with pale spots—and so are Fawn Darners. The genus name *Boyeria* is a tribute to the French entomologist Etienne Laurent Joseph Hippolyte Boyer de Fonscalombe (1772–1853). The species name *vinosa* can mean "full of wine" or "wine-colored"; it's not clear why this name was assigned to a brown dragonfly. Dragonfly expert Sid Dunkle speculates that the taxonomist who assigned the name was describing a preserved specimen that had become discolored.

Description: This is a fairly large dragonfly, about 2½ inches long. At a distance, in flight, males appear to be a uniform dark brown. Up close, you can see that they are actually a warm, rusty brown with elaborate markings. There are two large yellow spots on each side of the thorax, and rows of smaller yellow dots ornament the abdomen. The head appears large in relation to the body, and the face is greenish. The mostly clear wings have a small brown area at the base and brown stigmata at the tips. Female resemble males but are a little duller in color.

Habitat: This species is found around well-shaded, moderately fast-flowing streams and rivers, and also at the shady edges of windswept lakes.

When you'll see them: Fawn Darners have a long flight season, from summer to early fall.

Behavior: Fawn Darners most often spend their mornings settled on shaded perches, hanging in a vertical position. But they are still considered fliers, for in late afternoon they become especially active. As they cruise along streambanks and lakeshores, they trace an erratic, zigzag path, like wandering dogs nosing into every corner and stopping to inspect every obstacle.

The stocky, dark-colored nymphs hunker beneath stones in forest streams. Juveniles like to hang out in wooded areas, close to water. Adult males move to the edges of streams or lakes to commence their daily patrols, flying very low and slow over shallow water. They keep cruising well past twilight, when bats come out to join the chase for flying insects. The Fawn Darner has been described as a discriminating diner because sometimes, after capturing an insect, an individual can be seen to reject the prospective meal.

The male does not guard the female while she lays her eggs, which she places inside rotting wood or submerged water plants. Eggs that are laid in late summer may overwinter and not hatch until the following spring.

Similar species: The Springtime Darner is another big, brown, streamside dragonfly, but it flies earlier in the season. Also, on the thorax, where the Fawn Darner has two distinct spots, the Springtime Darner has two cream-colored stripes.

Black-shouldered Spinyleg *(Dromogomphus spinosus)*
Clubtail Family (Gomphidae)

About the name: All dragonflies have short spines on their legs that they use for catching insects. So why are members of the genus *Dromogomphus* the only ones that have earned the common name of spinylegs? Because their legs are even spinier than most. The hindlegs in particular are both unusually long and extra spiny; it almost looks as if the dragonfly has a couple of hairdresser's combs strapped to its thighs. The species name *spinosus*, Latin for "spiny" or "thorny," is an obvious choice. This species was given the common name black-shouldered because of the bold black stripes on the "shoulder" area of the thorax.

Description: Large, 2¼ inches long. The Black-shouldered Spinyleg's two distinctive features are the long spines on the hindlegs and the wide, black "shoulder bars" on the thorax. When they are juveniles, spinylegs have black bars on a shiny yellow thorax; as these dragonflies mature, the yellow thorax deepens in color to pale green. The abdomen is mostly black with some narrow yellow markings, the exact amount of yellow varying from individual to individual. The green eyes are set far apart in the pale yellow face, with the wide-eyed appearance typical of clubtails. The male's abdomen is slender, but with a bulging, clubbed tip; the female's abdomen, however, is barely clubbed.

Habitat: Clean, rock-strewn rivers with sandy bottoms and the gravelly margins of wind-whipped lakes.

When you'll see them: Depending on location, spinylegs may be seen in spring, summer, or fall.

Behavior: Typical of clubtails, these dragonflies are perchers. You may spot the males resting on rocks midstream, in a horizontal position. The wedge-shaped nymphs burrow into streambed sediments. When it's time to emerge, they crawl right up out of the water and continue crawling until they are well away from the water's edge, choosing a spot on a rock or a log to make their transformation.

You'll see the adult males cruising above a stretch of stream, holding steady about three feet above the water's surface. These dragonflies hold their bodies in a distinctive way while flying, with the abdomen tilted upward so that it is higher than the head. Mated pairs of Black-shouldered Spinylegs sometimes touch down in treetops to finish the act. Then the female lays her eggs unescorted, tapping her abdomen on the surface of the water.

Similar species: Two other species of spinylegs occur in the southeastern United States: the Southeastern Spinyleg and the Flag-Tailed Spinyleg. Although they superficially resemble the Black-shouldered Spinyleg, males of these two species can be identified by their orange clubtails.

Lancet Clubtail *(Gomphus exilis)*
Clubtail Family (Gomphidae)

About the name: The genus name *Gomphus* comes from the Greek word *gomphos*, meaning "bolt"—a special kind of arrow shot from a crossbow. The species name *exilis* is Latin for "slender" or "weak"; presumably the name was chosen because this is a comparatively slender member of the Clubtail family. A lancet is a medical tool used to draw blood; scientists who bestowed the English-language name chose this noun because the cerci on the tip of the male abdomen resemble sharp little lancet blades.

Description: Some clubtails are quite large, but Lancet Clubtails are medium-size, about 1³/₄ inches long. Like many clubtails, the male of this species has a dark brown thorax with narrow greenish-yellow stripes on the top and sides and a brown, club-shaped abdomen that is also marked with yellow. In this species, the yellow marks look like elongated, almost dagger-shaped triangles, one atop each segment. From a distance, the entire tip of the abdomen appears yellow. Females resemble males, but their thick abdomens are not club-tipped. The wings are clear and the face is green, with blue-gray eyes.

Habitat: Juveniles forage in open woodlands. Adults are found in quiet marshes, open ponds, lakes with sandy bottoms, and slow-moving streams.

When you'll see them: Lancet Clubtails fly from spring until fall.

Behavior: Like most clubtails, these are perchers. They tend to settle on the ground or on logs or rocks near the water's edge.

The nymphs like to burrow beneath the sediments that accumulate at the edge of a pond or stream. As adults, Lancet Clubtails scan for prey while perched, then make short flights to capture a meal. If a male is startled or feels threatened, he leaves his perch and flies in a characteristic pattern, zooming up and down, up and down in a steep roller-coaster pattern. It's thought that this behavior makes it hard for predators or competitors to follow his progress.

Females that are ready to lay eggs fly fast and low over the water, tapping the tip of the abdomen on the surface to deposit eggs.

Similar species: Clubtails can be hard to tell apart. Many species have the same general coloration: a dark body with greenish-yellow stripes. Some clubtail species can be identified only when you hold them in your hands and minutely examine their genitalia.

Twin-spotted Spiketail *(Cordulegaster maculata)*
Spiketail Family (Cordulegastridae)

About the name: The family Cordulegastridae gets its name from two Greek words: *kordylinus*, meaning "club-shaped," and *gaster*, meaning "belly." Spiketails don't have quite as big an abdominal bulge as clubtails, but their large abdomens do have a slightly clubbed appearance. The common name for the family, Spiketail, refers to the female's very prominent, spikelike ovipositor. The species name *maculata* can mean either "stained" or "spotted" in Latin; here it certainly refers to the pairs of spots that parade down the abdomen.

Description: Spiketails are quite large, more than 2³/₄ inches long. The paired yellow spots are unmistakable. Another distinctive feature is the dark thorax, which has two yellow stripes on each side. Males and females look alike, but the female's ovipositor sticks out well beyond the tip of the abdomen. Spiketails' coloration varies with geographic location. Northern populations have bright yellow spots on a black abdomen; southern populations have pale yellow spots on a brown abdomen. Also, northern populations have greenish eyes; southern populations have bluish eyes. As with all members of the Spiketail family, the two compound eyes meet in a point, not along a seam as with darners.

Habitat: Twin-spots can be found in the same habitat as trout: fast-flowing, clean woodland streams.

When you'll see them: Twin-spotted Spiketails are a spring species, meaning that large numbers emerge all at once, early in spring. This early emergence is possible because the nymphs have completed their development the previous fall; they overwinter in their final nymphal stage.

Behavior: Twin-spots are fliers, and adult males can be spotted making long patrols along the course of a stream or creek. When they do take a perch, it's by grasping a twig or stem so that their bodies hang down vertically from an overhead support. The hairy nymphs burrow into streambed sand or silt, choosing locations where pieces of decaying wood or fallen leaves have accumulated. Only their antennae stick up above the surface. Depending on the climate, it can take as long as three years for nymphs to complete their development. As adults, the males fly all day long, staying low near the surface of the stream as they hunt for females or for insects attracted to streamside plants. They carry their mates high in the treetops to mate. A female that is laying eggs hovers in an upright position over shallow water; then bobs up and down, plunging abdomen-first into the streambed again and again to insert her eggs in the sediments. The force of her descent can make her abdomen crumple in accordion folds.

Similar species: The Delta-spotted Spiketail is similar in appearance, but its spots are bigger, farther apart, and triangular.

Illinois River Cruiser *(Macromia illinoiensis)*
Cruiser Family (Macromiidae)

About the name: The genus name *Macromia* refers to the forked claws on the tips of all the legs. This family was dubbed the Cruisers because the males patrol unusually long beats, traveling as far as one hundred yards along a stream or river. Members of the group are sometimes referred to as Belted Skimmers because of the slanted yellow stripe that runs around the thorax, like a water-skier's lifebelt. This species was named the Illinois River Cruiser because the type specimen was collected in Illinois.

Description: Large, more than 2³/₄ inches long. The mature adults are big, black-and-yellow dragonflies with striking green eyes. Males and females are similar, but the male has a clubbed abdomen. The dark brown to black thorax is circled by a single slanted yellow stripe, or "belt." Near the tip of the dark abdomen is a large, bright yellow spot that's easy to see even when the dragonfly is in the air. If an Illinois River Cruiser ever stops cruising and perches, notice the long, spidery legs—they are characteristic of this family. So are the narrow, stiff-looking wings, the design of which helps these dragonflies fly very fast.

Habitat: Fast-flowing streams and, in northern areas, along the shorelines of large lakes.

When you'll see them: Spring to fall.

Behavior: Members of the Cruiser family are tireless fliers. Males tend to patrol their large streamside territories in early morning, zooming upstream and down like speedboats towing skiers around a reservoir. Juveniles are more likely than adults to stop and rest. These dragonflies like to spend the night in treetop perch sites, where they hang with their bodies held vertically.

When they are ready to emerge, the flat-bodied, long-legged, spiny nymphs crawl out of the water and well away from shore before settling on an emergence site. As adults, foraging river cruisers typically travel long distances, moving fast through open forest or coursing along a woodland road. They rarely stop to hover, but when the day warms up, they switch from steady, fast wingbeats to a more fluttering flight style.

Illinois River Cruisers sometimes join mixed-species swarms to feed on clouds of flying insects but tend to fly higher than most other species in the swarm. Scientists think that dragonflies flying at different heights in a swarm may be like wood-warblers foraging together in a mixed-species flock. Members of different species confine their searches to different parts of the trees, and this segmentation of the resource reduces the competition for prey.

Females stay away from the water until they are ready to mate, then pairs perch in trees while mating. Afterward, the females take off alone and cruise fast along the surface of the stream, tapping the tips of their abdomens against the surface every few yards to release their eggs.

Similar species: Stream Cruisers *(Didymops transversa)* have similar markings but tend to be a little smaller than Illinois River Cruisers. Several other traits distinguish Stream Cruisers from River Cruisers: the side stripes on the thorax are cream-colored, not yellow, in Stream Cruisers; Stream Cruisers have a lighter brown body color; and the spots on the abdomen are more numerous in Stream Cruisers, and cream-colored rather than yellow.

Common Baskettail *(Epitheca cynosura)*
Emerald Family (Corduliidae)

About the name: The species name *cynosura* comes from *cynosure*, Greek for "dog's tail." It's thought that this name refers to the way the male's cerci, or abdominal appendages, look when they are viewed from overhead. The two appendages curve outward, away from one another; squint and it looks like a dog's tail is wagging left and right.

Description: The Common Baskettail is considerably smaller than its royal relative, the Prince Baskettail, at only about 1$1/2$ inches in length. This is a solid-looking dragonfly with a very wide abdomen. Males and females are similar, with brown and noticeably furry thoraxes and brown abdomens with yellow markings up both sides. The forewings are clear, but the hindwings may have large, triangular brown marks at the base (members of some populations show this trait, while others do not). The eyes are brown in juveniles, but may be green or bluish green in adults.

Habitat: Perhaps one reason these dragonflies are called Common Baskettails is that you can find them around almost any aquatic habitat: lakes, marshes, ponds, swamps, and slow-moving streams and rivers. Foraging individuals will venture away from the water out over open fields, up forest roads, and even around parking lots.

When you'll see them: This is a spring species with a brief flight period. The exact timing of emergence varies with geographic location and local climate, but Common Baskettails typically emerge in late spring to early summer.

Behavior: Many dragonflies patrol at a deliberate pace, flying in a long, straight line like a helicopter on a mission. Common Baskettails look more like stunt planes as they zip around erratically. A feeding swarm of Common Baskettails puts on an exciting show. When these dragonflies do perch, they tend to choose a spot on a weedy stem, low to the ground, and they hold their bodies at an oblique angle to the substrate.

The nymphs are often found in habitats where fish also occur. But they avoid these predators by hiding among the leaves of water plants and in jumbled pond-bottom debris. Each adult male guards a territory along the water's edge and can sometimes be seen interrupting his patrol to hover in place over the water for several minutes at a time. Males feeding away from the water are less likely to hover. Males and females often hunt in large swarms, particularly in the afternoon. Common Baskettails are more pugnacious than their close relatives, the much larger Prince Baskettails, and have been spotted evicting their big cousins from desirable shoreline real estate.

The female's egg-laying behavior is typical of baskettails. First she squeezes out a string of eggs to form a ball on the tip of her abdomen; then she flies out over the water; finally, she dips her abdomen into the water to release the eggs, pressing one sticky end of the unraveling string onto a submerged plant.

Similar species: A number of baskettails are quite similar in appearance. The Common Baskettail is most often confused with the Mantled Baskettail, which is slightly smaller and has larger wing patches.

Prince Baskettail *(Epitheca princeps)*
Emerald Family (Corduliidae)

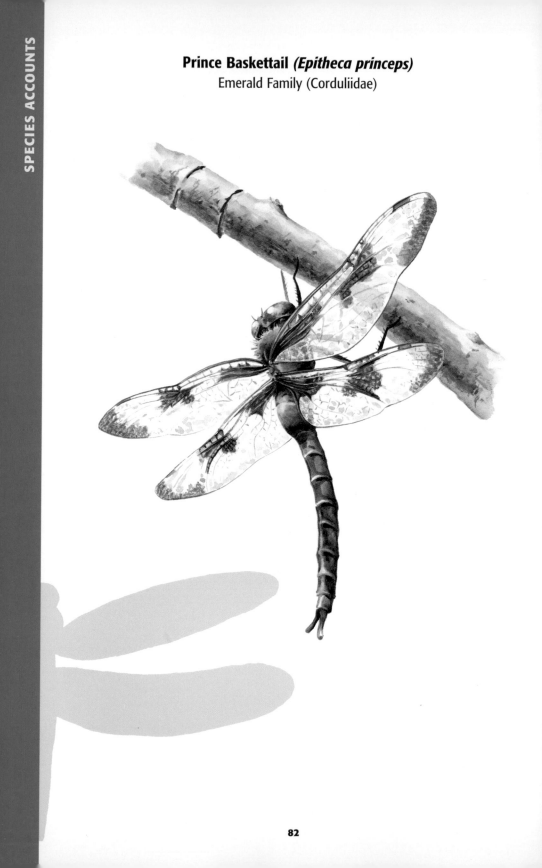

About the name: Baskettails are named for the way the female uses the tip of her abdomen (her "tail") like a basket to carry her clutch of eggs. As for the genus name, *Epitheca*, the Latin prefix *epi-* means "on top of," and *theca* is Latin for "house or case, chest, or box." Why this group of dragonflies has a name that means "on top of a box" is a bit of a mystery. The species name *princeps* means "ruler" or "chief"; this dragonfly deserves a lordly name, for compared with other baskettails, the Prince is quite large in size.

Description: Individuals within this species are usually large but can vary in size, from about 2$^1/_2$ inches to more than 3 inches long. There's an interesting geographic gradient with regard to body size: The biggest Prince Baskettails are found in southern states, smaller ones up north.

Most of the other very large dragonflies have clear wings, but the Prince Baskettail has boldly marked wings, so it is easy to recognize. The wing spots—irregular, lacy brown splotches—occur at the tip, middle, and base of each wing. Adult males have bright green eyes and a plain, dark-colored body. Females' eyes are a duller green than those of males, and juveniles' eyes are reddish brown. Also notice how the males' large claspers make a conspicuous "V" shape at the tip of the abdomen.

Habitat: Look for these majestic dragonflies around large lakes and slow-moving rivers.

When you'll see them: Prince Baskettails usually appear in summer.

Behavior: Energetic fliers, Prince Baskettails seem never to sit still. You may see them flying at any time of the day, from just before sunrise to just after sunset. At the rare times they do touch down, they adopt a tense posture, hanging beneath twigs with the abdomen lightly curled and the wings slightly raised.

Juveniles tend to feed along roads, so they often end up ornamenting the grillwork of passing cars. After adult males have claimed territories, they patrol their kingdoms at a stately pace, flying close to shore just above the water's surface, where they alternate between flapping and gliding flight. Like the Illinois River Cruiser, the Prince Baskettail sometimes joins mixed-species feeding swarms—and like the cruiser, it tends to take the high road, flying above other dragonfly species.

A mated female perches on a streamside plant to prepare her trademark egg ball. Curving her abdomen, she slowly squeezes out more than a thousand eggs. They stick together as they emerge, forming a bubbly ball that adheres to the tip of her abdomen. Next the female flies out unescorted over the water, searching for a place where submerged plants float close to the surface. She dips her abdomen in the water to release the blobby mass. Once immersed in water, the egg mass unravels into a thin string, perhaps 3 inches long. She anchors it by one sticky end to a water plant.

Similar species: Female Twelve-spotted Skimmers and female Common Whitetails have similarly patterned wings but stockier abdomens than female Prince Baskettails. Also, these two similar species are perchers, not fliers—and they perch low, not high in the treetops as the Prince Baskettail does.

Widow Skimmer *(Libellula luctuosa)*
Skimmer Family (Libellulidae)

About the name: Skimmers are aptly named—they do tend to skim low over the water. In Britain, some members of this group are called chasers, because of the way the males chase after each other. Some authors assert that the family name Libellulidae and the genus name *Libellula* come from the Latin *libellus*, meaning "little book." The idea is that when a dragonfly's wings spread flat, they look like an open book. Dragonfly expert Philip Corbet contests this idea, however. Tracing the name back through history, he has found that the genus name *Libella*, which is Latin for "a small, T-shaped scale," was first assigned to the hammerhead shark— a T-shaped animal if ever there was one. Then a sixteenth-century scholar, noting that damselfly nymphs were also T-shaped, assigned this same genus name to them. Subsequent scholars passed the name from damselflies to dragonflies. Members of the genus *Libellula* are sometimes called the King Skimmers because they are bigger than most other dragonflies and tend to dominate a pond, claiming the best perches. The species name is from *luctuosus*, Latin for "doleful," and the Widow Skimmer's black-marked wings do suggest mourning attire.

Description: These medium-size dragonflies are about 1³/₄ inches long with a 3-inch wingspan. Perhaps they should be called Widowers, not Widows: The males are the ones who wear full mourning garb. The key field mark is a wide, black band at the base of each wing, like a mourner's crepe armband. The rest of the mourning attire includes black eyes, a dusty gray thorax that is black on the sides, and a matching gray abdomen. Females and juveniles are a little more colorful, with bold yellow stripes down the sides of their dark abdomens. The male's black wing bands may be edged with white; females and juveniles also have black wing bands but lack the white edging.

Habitat: Widow Skimmers prefer still waters. They are found around permanent ponds, lakes, marshes, and occasionally slow-flowing streams.

When you'll see them: Widow Skimmers fly from late spring throughout the summer.

Behavior: Like most members of the Skimmer family, Widow Skimmers are perchers. Foraging adults claim perch sites in a field or meadow, settling on the tallest weeds and positioning their bodies at oblique angles to the stems. From these high perches, they sally out to capture flying insects.

Adult males that are ready to mate will cluster together in small adjoining territories and establish a kind of pecking order among themselves; the dominant male in the neighborhood has the best chance of claiming a mate. The female dips her abdomen into the water again and again as she lays her eggs. The male may guard her, but if the population is dense, he will go elsewhere, skirmishing with other males. In between their territorial patrolling flights, male Widow Skimmers perch for long periods on emergent pond plants. Because the males return repeatedly to the same perch, they are easy to spot, and you can spend a good, long time examining their field marks.

Similar species: Black Saddlebags superficially resemble Widow Skimmers but have a black patch at the base of each hindwing, rather than black bands on both pairs of wings. Young male Common Whitetails also resemble Widow Skimmers but have a black band at the center of each wing, rather than at the base.

Common Whitetail (*Libellula lydia*; also known as *Plathemis lydia*)
Skimmer Family (Libellulidae)

MALE

About the name: It's easy to see where this skimmer gets the name Whitetail. As the male matures, he develops a chalk white coating all over his plump abdomen.

The species name *Lydia* was probably chosen as a tribute to some entomologist's wife, mother, or muse, but the identity of the woman who inspired the name is not known.

Description: Common Whitetails are medium-size dragonflies, about 1³/₄ inches long with a 2³/₄-inch wingspan. Their wide, dark wing bands and thick abdomens make them look bigger than they really are. Males are spectacular and very easy to identify. When mature, they have dark brown eyes in a dark brown face, a dark thorax, and a bright, chalk white abdomen. Their wing pattern is equally distinctive: a narrow dark-brown stripe at the base of each wing and a wide brown band across the center of each wing. Females look quite different from males, with a brown thorax and abdomen. Slanted, pale-yellow markings on the sides of the abdomen give it a saw-toothed appearance. Females have three large, dark spots on their wings, located at the base, middle, and tip.

Habitat: Expect to see Common Whitetails in the same places you see Twelve-spotted Skimmers. Both species like still water, so you'll often see them around warm, weedy ponds, but they can also be found around marshes and sluggish streams. They tolerate somewhat polluted water and disturbed sites, and adults are attracted to exposed mud.

When you'll see them: This widespread dragonfly has a long flight season, from early spring into autumn.

FEMALE

Behavior: This is a well-studied species, so scientists know a lot about its behavior. Busily defending their territories, males may spend well over half their time in flight. Still, Common Whitetails are considered perchers, because their flights are fairly short and interrupted by frequent rest stops, during which they perch on weeds, rocks, fallen logs, or even on the ground. You'll often see one touch down right in the middle of the road or flat on a boat dock. Move slowly, and you can get very close for a good look.

The nymphs are burrowers. Adult males claim a territory at the water's edge and may return to the same site repeatedly for as many as ten days in a row. There's a pecking order among males around a pond; the dominant male raises his white abdomen like a flag and darts at other males, who lower their abdomens as a sign of submission. When a male claims a female, the pair hovers over the water to mate. It's all over in about three seconds.

Among dragonflies as a group, the speed at which eggs are laid is a function of abdomen size, and the female Common Whitetail, with her very fat abdomen, is especially speedy—she can expel close to two thousand eggs in a minute as she taps her abdomen on the water's surface. To give you a sense of how fast this is, the Ruby Meadowhawk, a much smaller, slimmer dragonfly, lays fewer than eighty eggs a minute. The male Common Whitetail may hover nearby while the female releases her eggs, or he may be distracted by another male who is challenging his rights to the territory—or perhaps the distraction is the chance to mate with another female. Because Common Whitetails can mate so fast, the male is often able to take a second mate and then guard two females at once.

Similar species: Female Twelve-spotted Skimmers and female Common Whitetails look much alike, both having brown-spotted wings with dark tips. However, Common Whitetails are notably smaller than Twelve-spots, and have spots along the edge of the abdomen rather than a yellow stripe.

Twelve-spotted Skimmer *(Libellula pulchella)*
Skimmer Family (Libellulidae)

About the name: This species has three black spots on each of its four wings, hence Twelve-spotted Skimmer. Just to make things confusing, though, these dragonflies are sometimes called Ten-spots. That's for the number of *white* spots on a mature male's wings—two white spots on each forewing and three on each hindwing. The species name speaks for itself: *Pulchellus* is Latin for "pretty."

Description: These are large, stout-bodied dragonflies, about 2 inches long with a 3^1/$_2$-inch wingspan. The male has distinctive black and white spots on its wings, whereas the female has black wing spots only. Adult males are brown on the face and thorax. As juveniles, they also have brown abdomens with yellow side stripes as well as two narrow yellow stripes on each side of the thorax. As the male matures, his side stripes fade and his abdomen develops a chalky, bluish gray coating. Females look like juvenile males.

Habitat: Twelve-spotted Skimmers frequent shallow, nutrient-rich ponds and lakes with marshy edges, as well as slow-moving streams. They feed in upland fields, well away from the water.

When you'll see them: Twelve-spots are most numerous in early summer but emerge all season long.

Behavior: This is another perching skimmer. When foraging in open fields, Twelve-spots choose tall weeds to perch on while they scan for prey. On cool mornings, they sunbathe to warm up; they perch facing the sun and lift their abdomens to catch more rays. After a pair mates, the female flies off alone to lay her eggs. She hovers just above the surface over an area of shallow water that is thick with submerged vegetation, tapping the tip of her abdomen into the water again and again, sometimes striking the water so hard that she sends a droplet flying. Twelve-spot nymphs are burrowers.

There's some evidence that Twelve-spot populations along the Atlantic coast are migratory, and you may notice swarms moving northward or southward in spring or fall.

Similar species: Female Twelve-spotted Skimmers resemble female Common Whitetails, but Twelve-spots are larger. They may also be confused with Prince Baskettails, though Twelve-spots have much thicker abdomens.

Calico Pennant *(Celithemis elisa)*
Skimmer Family (Libellulidae)

About the name: Members of this genus are called pennants because they resemble festive holiday pennants as they perch at the tips of tall weed stems and flutter their colorful wings. The genus name *Celithemis* includes the Greek prefix *celi*, meaning "spot," a reference to the spotted wings that ornament members of this group. The Calico Pennant's spots are orange and brown and vary in size and color, like the spots on a calico cat. You might also hear these dragonflies called Valentine Pennants. That's for the red markings on the male's abdomen, which look like a chain of tiny hearts.

Description: Pennants are a little bigger than their relatives the meadowhawks; they are about 1 1/2 inches long with a 2 1/4-inch wingspan. The male has a black thorax with dull red stripes and a black abdomen marked with a distinctive series of red triangles. Both sets of wings have small, dark spots at the tips and middle. In addition, the hindwings have large, irregular, red and brown spots at the base. Females and juvenile males are brown on both thorax and abdomen, and they have yellow rather than red triangles on the abdomen.

Habitat: Pennants like ponds and marshes with tall water plants; they also forage in neighboring fields.

When you'll see them: Calico Pennants fly throughout the summer.

Behavior: These perchers like to settle on the very tips of tall plants, where they adopt a horizontal pose and look like miniature flags blowing in the wind. When male Calico Pennants take up stations on tall plants near the edge of the pond, they don't position themselves so they are looking out over the pond, the way most dragonflies do. Instead, they face away from the water so they can scan the fields nearby for incoming females.

The slender, greenish, delicate-looking nymphs are known for their ability to survive in ponds that support fish; they escape predation by hiding in dense stands of water plants and amid jumbled debris on the bottom. These nymphs require clean water, so their presence in a pond indicates good water quality.

Males do not defend territories; they are most active in the morning, when they flutter from perch to perch. Females lay eggs while flying in tandem, dipping their abdomens into the water over barely submerged plants.

Similar species: Halloween Pennants are somewhat similar to Calico Pennants but have amber-tinted wings and lack the large, multicolored patch at the base of the hindwing.

Halloween Pennant (Celithemis eponina)
Skimmer Family (Libellulidae)

About the name: Halloween colors—orange and black—give the Halloween Pennant its common name. *Epona*, the root of the species name, was the Roman goddess of horses. It's not known why some scientist long ago assigned that name to this dragonfly.

Description: Halloween Pennants are small, but a little larger than their relatives the Calico Pennants; they are about 1½ inches long, with a 3-inch wingspan.

The Halloween Pennant is especially easy to identify in the field—its wings are so distinctive. Juveniles have amber-tinted wings; this color deepens to an orangey red in the wings of the adults. Both sets of wings are heavily marked with brown spots and bands, and the stigmata at the tips of the wing are a bright orange-red. Both thorax and abdomen are dark in color, and the adult male has a reddish stripe down the middle of the abdomen.

Habitat: These dragonflies breed in ponds, lakes, and marshes, but you are most likely to see them when they are foraging away from the water, on nearby grassy slopes.

When you'll see them: Despite the autumnal name, Halloween Pennants fly in summer.

Behavior: Like other pennants, these are perchers that like to settle at the very tips of tall plants, holding their bodies in a horizontal position. While perched, they hold their wings in a distinctive way. The two sets of wings are tilted in different planes, with the hindwings held horizontal but the forewings angled up toward vertically. It's thought that in this position the dark wing spots help to shade the body. On hot days, you are especially likely to see Halloween Pennants taking the obelisk position: head down, abdomen up, and wings slightly raised. In flight, Halloween Pennants flutter along, looking more like butterflies than dragonflies.

The nymphs are quite spiny. Halloween Pennants are most active in the mornings. The females lay their eggs while flying in tandem with the males and often do this work on days when high winds keep other dragonflies from flying.

Similar species: The male Calico Pennant is superficially similar but lacks the wide bands at the tips of both sets of wings. The female Eastern Amberwing resembles the Halloween Pennant in that it has very colorful wings, but it is much smaller.

Slaty Skimmer *(Libellula incesta)*
Skimmer Family (Libellulidae)

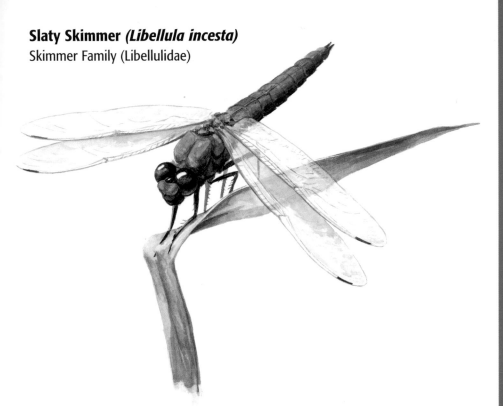

About the name: Seen from a distance, adult male Slaty Skimmers look black, but up close they are a beautiful dark slate blue. The species name *incesta* is from the Latin *incesto*, which means to "defile, pollute, or dishonor" and implies lewd or unchaste behavior. The nineteenth-century zoologist who first described the species gave it this name because he thought it looked like a hybrid that had resulted from a mating between two other species that have mostly blue bodies, the Great Blue Skimmer and the Bar-winged Skimmer. But in fact, this is a true species, not a hybrid.

Description: This is another large skimmer, 2 inches long with a 3-inch wingspan. Slaty Skimmers have been called "the crows of the dragonfly world" because they look black and you see them everywhere. Other than the all-over slate blue color, here are some other field marks to notice: The wings are clear; the eyes are dark brown in a black face; and seen in silhouette, the broad abdomen is noticeably tapered at the tip. Juvenile males and females are not slate blue; the thorax is brown with yellow side stripes, and the yellow abdomen has a wide black stripe down the middle. Females fade to an overall gray color as they age.

Habitat: These skimmers like still waters in wooded areas. You're most likely to see them around muddy-bottomed ponds and lakes.

When you'll see them: Slaty Skimmers fly all summer long.

Behavior: Slaty Skimmers are perchers. They'll pick the tallest cattail or weed in a patch of sun and position their bodies at an oblique angle to this vertical perch site. Thus ensconced, they may sit still for hours.

Foraging adults head away from the water to hunt for insects along forest edges. Back at the pond or lake, the males defend territories by perching on tall stems along the shoreline. They're most active early in the morning. Like Twelve-spotted Skimmers, they defend their territories by flying loops around intruders.

Females show up near the water only when they are ready to mate, and this may happen even before they have developed their mature adult color pattern of all-over gray. After mating, which is quick, the female lays her eggs while the male guards nearby.

Similar species: The male Slaty Skimmer is the only large, dark-all-over dragonfly in the eastern United States. Other species with completely dark bodies are much smaller. Identifying the female Slaty Skimmer is not so easy; the females of several related species, including the Great Blue Skimmer, look quite similar to female Slaties.

Eastern Pondhawk *(Erythemis simplicicollis)*
Skimmer Family (Libellulidae)

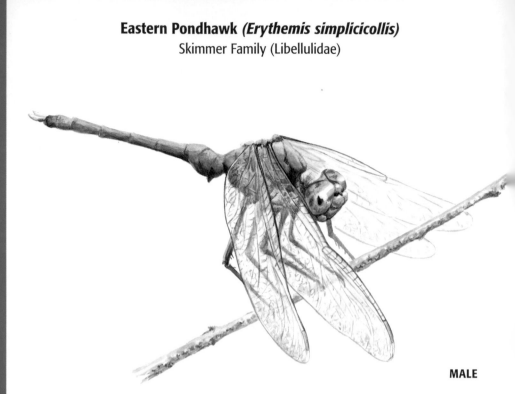

MALE

About the name: Pondhawk is an apt common name for members of this group, as these dragonflies hang around ponds and are voracious hunters. The genus name is from the Greek word *erythema*, which describes a red flush on the skin. This seems like a funny choice of name for a pale blue dragonfly, but a number of closely related species—all of them living in the tropics—are indeed red. The species name *simplicicollis* is made up of two Latin words meaning "simple neck" and refers to the prothorax, the area of the thorax closest to the head—where the neck would be if dragonflies had necks. Experts who look closely at such things have concluded that the pondhawk's prothorax is simple in structure compared with, say, the prothorax of a meadowhawk, which is hairy and complicated in shape.

Description: Eastern Pondhawks are medium-size, about 1³/₄ inches long. The adult male can be identified by his simple color scheme: a green head contrasting with a pale blue body. Juveniles and females are bright pea-soup green all over—this is an unusual coloration for dragonflies—with broad, black ornamental stripes on the abdomen. Both males and females have clear wings.

As the juvenile males mature, their green-and-black pattern is gradually covered up by a chalky blue coating. This coating first develops on the abdomen, then spreads to the thorax. The color change happens over a period of days and occurs faster when the weather is warm and when the dragonfly is well fed.

FEMALE

Habitat: Pondhawks like ponds, especially ponds with plenty of duckweed, water lilies, and other aquatic plants. They can also be found around quiet lakes, and they tolerate slightly brackish water.

When you'll see them: Eastern Pondhawks fly all summer long.

Behavior: These are classic perchers that favor low perch sites. You'll typically see Eastern Pondhawks resting in a horizontal position on the ground, on floating debris, or on a fallen log or rock. They also land on flat water lily leaves.

Eastern Pondhawks share a foraging strategy with cowbirds and Cattle Egrets: They go after the insects stirred up by big mammals such as cows, horses, or people walking through tall grass. They are expert hunters and have been called our most ferocious dragonflies, unhesitatingly attacking prey that's as big as or bigger than they are—including damselflies, other dragonflies, and even other pondhawks.

Even when you're too far away to see any field marks, you can identify male pondhawks by their distinctive "cartwheel contests." During these exciting chases, two males take turns swooping over or under each other in a fast, leapfrogging flight.

Females spend less time near the water than males do. When they are ready to lay eggs, they hover over patches of algae and dip their abdomens downward repeatedly. Some eggs wash off into the water with each dip.

Similar species: Juvenile Eastern Pondhawks resemble Green Darners in their blue-and-green color scheme, but they are much smaller than the darners and lack the dark stripe down the top of the abdomen. The adult male Eastern Pondhawk superficially resembles the male Blue Dasher, but the pondhawk is pale blue all over, whereas the dasher has a dark thorax and a dark tip to the abdomen.

Blue Dasher *(Pachydiplax longipennis)*
Skimmer Family (Libellulidae)

About the name: If you've ever tried to catch a Blue Dasher in a net, you know where these dragonflies get their name; they take off fast from their perches and dash about in a way that makes them very hard to catch. The genus name is a combination of two words: *Pachy* means "thick" and probably was chosen to describe the female's stout abdomen; *diplax* is Greek for "mantle" or "cloak." The species name *longipennis* means "long wing"; the female Blue Dasher has a comparatively short abdomen, which makes her wings look very long.

Description: Blue Dashers vary in size from small to medium-size, about 1 to 1³/₄ inches long. Dashers emerging in spring tend to be larger than late-emerging individuals. The adult male's eyes are amazing: they are very large and a glistening metallic green that stands out against a white face. His abdomen is also distinctive, pale powder blue all over, with a dark tip. The thorax is brown or black, with yellow zebra stripes that fade with age. The wings sometimes have an amber tint, although the extent of the color can vary. The attractive female looks totally unlike the male, with reddish brown eyes, a dark thorax, and a dark abdomen with double yellow dashes down its length.

Habitat: Nymphs of this species tolerate water that is low in oxygen and will live in disturbed or somewhat polluted environments. As a result, you'll find Blue Dashers around almost any still water, including ponds, marshes, swamps, and the sluggish backwaters of slow-moving streams and rivers.

When you'll see them: Blue Dashers fly from early to late summer.

Behavior: The Blue Dasher is a percher, and when perched it often takes a characteristic stance, with the body held horizontally and the wings pushed forward and downward, as if the dragonfly is caught in an invisible tailwind. Holding the wings in this position probably helps create shade for the thorax on hot days. Both males and females select good feeding perches on twigs or rocks and return to them with clockwork regularity; they defend their choice seats vigorously if other dragonflies try to settle there.

Like Eastern Amberwings, Blue Dashers often obelisk, doing little dragonfly headstands in an effort to stay cool. And like Common Whitetails, another species with a conspicuously pale abdomen, Blue Dashers often defend their lakeside territories by raising their abdomens in threatening displays. Territory owners also dart out to hover close to intruders; as the confrontation escalates, each of the dragonflies jockeys to get below the other, the better to force it up and away.

The female lays her eggs in the usual skimmer way, by tapping her abdomen against the water, but whereas most female skimmers trace an undulating flight path—rising, then descending to make their taps—female dashers fly along on a steady, even plane, very low to the water, so that they need only lower their abdomens a bit to deposit eggs from time to time. While egg laying is going on, the male may either perch or hover nearby.

Similar species: With their pale blue abdomens, male Blue Dashers resemble Eastern Pondhawks. You can identify a Blue Dasher, however, by its striped thorax and dark abdominal tip; the pondhawk has a plain blue thorax and abdomen. It's possible to mistake a Blue Dasher for a male Common Whitetail, whose white abdomen may look chalky blue, but the male whitetail has a wide, well-defined dark stripe down the middle of each wing, whereas the dasher lacks this stripe. Blue Dashers do sometimes have dark, smoky marks on the wings, but typically these marks are at the base of the wing and on the outer half, not in the middle of the wing as with whitetails.

Wandering Glider *(Pantala flavescens)*
Skimmer Family (Libellulidae)

About the name: Their long-distance migrations and skill at gliding flight are what earned this species the lovely name Wandering Glider. The genus name *Pantala* means "all wings" and refers to the unusually long, wide wings; the species name *flavescens* is Latin for "yellow" and describes this dragonfly's golden body. Members of the genus *Pantala* are also called the Rainpool Gliders, for their habit of laying eggs in the temporary ponds and puddles that form after spring rains.

Description: Wandering Gliders are medium-size dragonflies, about 1³/₄ inches long, but with an impressive 3-inch wingspan. From a distance the adult male appears golden yellow overall; up close, you can see the yellow-orange face and the complicated dark markings on his abdomen. The eyes are deep chestnut brown. Both pairs of wings are clear, although the hindwings may be tinted brown at the tips. The wings are unusually wide at the base—an adaptation for gliding flight. Females resemble males but are duller in color.

Habitat: Wandering Gliders forage away from the water, over open fields and even above asphalt parking lots. When it's time to lay eggs, they breed in the temporary ponds left by heavy spring rains. Any small body of water will do—these dragonflies have been spotted depositing their eggs in puddles about 2 feet square. They've also been known to mistake a car's shiny finish or hot, shimmering asphalt for a puddle of water.

When you'll see them: Wandering Gliders fly from summer through early fall. In spring, the members of southern populations fly north to breed. The nymphs complete their development quickly and emerge as adults the same summer, to wing their way south in the fall.

Behavior: The Wandering Glider is perfectly adapted for sustained flight and typically mixes short bouts of flapping with long periods of gliding. When it does take a break from flying, this dragonfly likes to grab hold of a horizontal or angled twig or branch and let its body hang down vertically.

As you might expect of a species adapted to breeding in puddles, Wandering Glider nymphs grow unusually fast; after all, they need to complete their development and emerge as adults before their home evaporates. Adults often feed in large swarms, and a group of gliders will "mob," or collectively attack, a larger dragonfly, much the way sparrows gang up to scare away a crow or hawk.

Equipped with big wings and able to store large amounts of fat in their wide abdomens, adult Wandering Gliders travel long distances in search of new ponds. They form swarms not just to feed, but also when migrating—one particularly massive migratory swarm is reported to have covered 13 square miles. In their seasonal migrations, these dragonflies may travel hundreds or even thousands of miles, and they have even been spotted touching down on ships far out to sea. After mating takes place, the male and female fly in tandem while she lays her eggs.

Similar species: The Spot-winged Glider, a closely related Rainpool Glider species, looks a lot like the Wandering Glider but can be distinguished by its brownish color and by the dark spot (not always easy to see) at the base of the hindwing. The two species often fly together, and they have very similar habits. Female and juvenile meadowhawks superficially resemble Wandering Gliders—they are orange-yellow all over, and they spend much of their time foraging over meadows; however, meadowhawks are much smaller than gliders and spend more time perching.

Eastern Amberwing
(Perithemis tenera)
Skimmer Family (Libellulidae)

MALE

About the name: The male's transparent wings, tinted gemstone amber, give the Eastern Amberwing its common name. The genus name *Perithemis* is derived from Themis, the guardian of peace and justice in Greek mythology. A number of other genera in the Skimmer family pay homage to Themis; North America also has *Celithemis, Crocothemis, Dythemis, Erythemis, Macrothemis, Nannothemis, Orthemis, Paltothemis*, and *Plathemis*. Perhaps taxonomists who assigned these names drew a connection between this ancient goddess and dragonflies because Justice is often depicted holding a scale or balance, and early taxonomists described dragonfly nymphs as resembling a T-shaped balance. The species name *Tenera* is Latin for "tender, delicate, or soft," and implies youth.

Description: This is the second-smallest North American dragonfly—it's less than an inch long. Only the Elfin Skimmer is smaller. Males have clear, honey-colored wings with red stigmata at the tips. Their overall color scheme is a symphony of harvest colors: the head is orange to rust-colored, with brown eyes; the brown thorax has yellow spots on the sides; and the fairly stout abdomen is patterned in shades of brown with pale, narrow rings demarcating the segments. Females also have a ringed abdomen, but the wings usually are not amber all over; instead, they show irregular light brown or amber patches on a clear background.

From a distance, these small, golden yellow dragonflies look more like wasps than dragonflies. Perched on a flowerhead, they complete the impression by waving their wings and waggling their abdomens in a waspy way. This expert impersonation probably confers some advantages; predators such as birds that might snap up a tiny dragonfly will think twice about tackling a wasp.

Habitat: Eastern Amberwings are found around ponds and slow streams. The nymphs seem to tolerate less-than-perfectly-clean water.

FEMALE

When you'll see them: Eastern Amberwings fly from summer into early autumn.

Behavior: Eastern Amberwings are perchers. Around the water, males choose low perch sites on shoreline plants. When they fly, they stay low over the water. Feeding over fields, away from water, Eastern Amberwings look weak as they fly, and they stop often to perch on open flowers. On very hot, sunny days, these dragonflies often assume the obelisk stance, with the head down and abdomen up, to help them stay cool.

When it's time to emerge, nymphs often choose dead tree stumps as the site for their transformation. Adult males heading out on patrol from their shoreline perches tend to fly low over the water. Should another male approach, a territory holder will defend his turf by flying fast and straight at the intruder, flapping those colorful wings as if to shoo the other dragonfly away.

Courtship displays are much more common among damselflies than among dragonflies, but the Eastern Amberwing is one of the few dragonfly species that does work hard to woo a mate. If a male Amberwing sees a female approaching, he flies out toward her and, swaying from side to side, leads the way back toward his territory. On home ground, he hovers in place over the water with his abdomen conspicuously raised as if to draw her attention to some floating vegetation that she should find very appropriate for egg laying. If the female agrees, the two fly off and find a shoreline perch where they mate. Then the male again leads the female back to the egg-laying site. At this point, he may leave her alone, hover close by, or hold on to her as she dabs small clusters of eggs on pond scum or sticks that are floating at the water's surface. The egg clusters explode as they touch the water, distributing the eggs over the bottom.

Similar species: Three amberwing species occur in North America, but the Eastern Amberwing is the only species found in the Northeast.

Yellow-legged Meadowhawk *(Sympetrum vicinum)*
Skimmer Family (Libellulidae)

About the name: Plenty of dragonflies like to forage over open meadows, well away from water; meadowhawks are a large and colorful group of dragonflies named for this habit. The genus name *Sympetrum* means "with rocks" and probably refers to this species' habit of basking on rocks early in the day to warm up. The species name *vicinum* is Latin for "neighborhood" or "vicinity."

Description: All meadowhawks are small. This one is only about 1¼ inches long, with a wingspan of about 2 inches. If Slaty Skimmers are the crows of the dragonfly world, these little beauties are the Northern Cardinals. The adult males are bright red all over—red face, red eyes, red thorax, red abdomen, even coordinating red stigmata on the tips of the clear wings. Despite their name, mature adult males do not have yellow legs; the legs are red or red-brown. Only the juveniles and females have yellow legs—indeed, juveniles are yellow all over. (Adult females have olive-brown or reddish abdomens.)

Habitat: When they're foraging, Yellow-legs hang out in open meadows and clearings, far from the nearest water. This species is found around a variety of aquatic habitats: permanent and temporary ponds, lakes, bogs, marshes, and even slow-moving streams.

When you'll see them: Yellow-legged Meadowhawks are late-season dragonflies. They don't start emerging until July. They're also the last dragonflies still flying in autumn. You may see them as late as November or December even in the cold Northeast.

Behavior: Yellow-legged Meadowhawks tend to be perchers. When the weather is cool, they favor low perch sites—wide, flat leaves; rocks; fallen logs; or the ground. Here, resting in a horizontal position, they soak up the sun. Yellow-legs have also been seen perching on warm heaps of compost. By the water, adult males perch on low vegetation. They especially like to perch on light-colored surfaces. They seem less skittish than most dragonflies and have developed a reputation as friendly dragonflies that will land right on your T-shirt. Observers have reported seeing whole lines of meadowhawks sitting in a row on fence rails, all of them facing the same way like swallows on a wire. In flight, Yellow-legged Meadowhawks are slow—slow enough that with practice, some dragonfly enthusiasts can catch them with their bare hands.

Nymphs, like adults, are small and slender. They burrow in soft sediments. Juveniles take several weeks to achieve sexual maturity; during this time, they hang out in wooded areas.

The female lays eggs while flying in tandem with the male. The sight of one tandem pair seems to attract others, so that soon there's a little orgy of egg laying going on. Females dip their abdomens in water to make the eggs sticky, then tap the eggs out onto damp moss or a muddy bank, where the eggs will overwinter. The nymphs don't hatch out until the next spring, when the water rises to cover them or when spring rains wash them down into the water. In cold northern areas, Yellow-legs migrate south for the winter.

Similar species: The male Yellow-legs is the only plain red meadowhawk; in other species, males are red but have black triangles on the sides of the abdomen, or other dark markings. To identify females, look at the underside of the tip of the abdomen. The ovipositor flares in a distinctive trumpet shape.

Black Saddlebags *(Tramea lacerata)*
Skimmer Family (Libellulidae)

About the name: In author Philip Pullman's popular books for children, fairylike beings use tame dragonflies as winged mounts. Imagine dragonfly steeds tacked up for long-distance travel, and you can see where Saddlebag Gliders get their name: the large, rounded spots on the hindwings resemble tiny sets of saddlebags. Some sources call members of this group the Dancing Gliders because a mated pair performs a graceful *pas de deux* while the female lays her eggs. The genus name *Tramea* is Latin for "perineum," and is thought to refer to the prominent split plate visible on the underside of the female's abdomen. The species name *lacerata* means "torn" and describes the ragged edges of the hindwing spots.

Description: This is a large dragonfly, 2 inches long or more. Males and females look quite similar. Both sexes have mostly black bodies and unusually wide hindwings. Each wing is marked at the base with a large, rounded, ragged-edged black spot. When the wings are raised, the half-round spots give Black Saddlebags a hunchbacked appearance. Females and juveniles have yellow faces, whereas the adult male's face is dark. Light cream to yellow spots on the abdomen fade with age.

Habitat: Black Saddlebags frequent still water, including ditches, ponds, lakes, and marshes. This species does best in habitats that lack fish.

When you'll see them: Black Saddlebags fly from summer through fall.

Behavior: Black Saddlebags are strong fliers. When they do perch, they usually hang vertically from the underside of branches or twigs, but will also pose horizontally at the tips of branches the way most members of this family do. The "saddlebags" on the hindwings seem to serve as an impromptu parasol; on very hot days, a perched Black Saddlebags will let its abdomen droop into the shade created by the big black spots.

Some populations are migratory. The winged adults fly north in spring, mate, and lay eggs. Nymphs complete their development in a single summer, emerge, and wing their way south in autumn. On their southbound migrations, Black Saddlebags have been seen joining mixed-species swarms that also include Common Green Darners and Variegated Meadowhawks. Black Saddlebags often forage in swarms and are more active in the morning than the afternoon. A lone male may claim, defend, and patrol an entire small pond.

Mating takes place while the pair perches in a shrub or tree near the water. Afterward, they perform the graceful, coordinated flight that gave them the name of Dancing Gliders. In the tandem position—with the male holding the female's head in his claspers—the two fly out from their mating perch. He releases her just as she dips her abdomen in the water, hovers above her as she releases her eggs, then quickly gathers her back into his embrace. The pair flies on to the next spot, where the dance steps repeat. This romantic-looking waltz actually brings two advantages for the male. By flying with her, he guards his partner from the advances of other males. And by releasing her just before she touches the water's surface, he reduces his risk of being snapped up by a fish.

Similar species: This is the only saddlebag species with light spots on the abdomen. Carolina Saddlebags are similar in overall appearance, but they are red where this species is black; the Carolina Saddlebags may look black when backlit by the sun, however. Female Widow Skimmers also are similar looking, with large black spots at the base of the hindwings, but the yellow markings on the abdomen of the Widow Skimmer are more prominent.

Spot-winged Glider
(Pantala hymenaea)
Skimmer Family (Libellulidae)

About the name: A dark spot on the base of each hindwing gives this dragonfly its common name. The species name *hymenaea* means "skin" or "membrane."

Description: Like the Wandering Glider, this is a medium-size dragonfly with very long wings. Males and females are quite similar in appearance, both having a brown thorax and abdomen. However, the male has reddish brown eyes in a reddish face; the female, in contrast, has a yellow face. The small, dark spot at the base of each wide hindwing is not always easy to see in the field.

Habitat: Spot-winged Gliders are found in the same places as Wandering Gliders, breeding in temporary pools or ponds and feeding over fields and meadows.

When you'll see them: Spot-winged Gliders are active from spring through fall. Their seasonal migration patterns are like those of the Wandering Glider, but Spot-wings show up in northern areas a little earlier than their relatives.

Behavior: Like Wandering Gliders, Spot-wings are expert fliers, capable of gliding on and on. Their smooth progress is interrupted periodically by bouts of flapping flight, although Spot-winged Gliders don't seem to hover as much as Wandering Gliders do. Spot-wings often join Wandering Gliders in feeding swarms and may stay in the air all day long, pursuing prey. They perch by hanging from a twig or branch with the body in a vertical position.

Just like their cousins, Spot-winged Glider nymphs complete their development very quickly. Adult males defend large territories. Migratory swarms are especially common along the Atlantic coast. Females usually lay their eggs while flying tandem with males, but they sometimes do their work alone.

Similar species: Spot-winged Gliders resemble Wandering Gliders but look more brown overall; Wanderers are more golden yellow. The various saddlebag species resemble Spot-wings but have hindwing spots that are larger or different in shape.

5

Watching Dragonflies

It's a warm summer day, sunny, calm, and windless—in short, the perfect day to get outside and see some dragonflies. What should you take on your dragonfly field trip? A few basic items will make your dragonfly-watching expedition more pleasant and more productive:

- Map of the area
- Drinking water and snacks
- Sunscreen and hat
- Field guide
- Close-focusing binoculars
- Notebook and pencil or waterproof pen
- Insect net and 8x or 10x hand lens (optional)
- Camera with macro lens (optional)

A first-aid kit may also come in handy. Put on sunscreen before you leave, and wear a hat: Dragonflies are usually found in sunny places, and many species are most active at midday, when the sun's rays are most harmful to human skin. Also take along raingear in case the weather changes.

Since you are likely to be around water, wear shoes that can get wet. Depending on the water temperature and the terrain you plan to navigate, you might consider wearing river sandals, knee-high rubber boots, or an old pair of sneakers. With water-worthy footgear, you can wade slowly along a shoreline—a great way to see dragonflies.

Field Notes

Taking notes on field trips may seem like extra work at first, but you'll find it's valuable in several ways. For one thing, note taking encourages you to observe dragonflies and their surroundings more carefully. And when you're more focused, you'll learn faster and remember better. Use a pencil or water-proof pen to write your field notes. Waterproof paper is handy but not essential. Some folks prefer to use a portable tape recorder or digital recorder.

At a minimum, record what species you see on each trip, along with details on their appearance and behavior. Also try to estimate how many of each species you see. You may want to make some sketches, too, or snap pictures with a camera.

Your field notes will be even more valuable if you also record some basic field data. One especially useful piece of data is the precise location where you are making the observations. Consult your map and jot down the state, county, and nearest town or city, as well as the names of nearby roads and other landmarks, such as the closest lake, pond, or stream. Other essential field data include the date of your field trip; the time of day you are making your observations; and details about the weather. A local radio station should provide information on air temperature, relative humidity, and windspeed. Also note the amount of cloud cover: Is the sky 100 percent covered with clouds? 75 percent? 50 percent? 25 percent? Completely clear?

What type of habitat are you visiting—meadow, forest, stream, pond, marsh? If you are familiar with plant names, make note of the dominant vege-tation—whatever types of trees, grasses, and other plants are most common.

Many of these factors are clues to the identity of the dragonflies you see. Some dragonflies start flying early in the day; others are active later in the day. Different species prefer different habitats: fast-flowing water or still water; lush aquatic vegetation or crystalline waters. By noting more than just field marks, you'll have more data to help verify the ID.

Dragonflies have been so little studied that your field trip observations could yield useful new information. Even as a beginning observer of drag-onflies, you have the potential to make a significant contribution to basic sci-ence and to dragonfly conservation efforts. By recording what species you see and the accompanying field data, you may help expand the knowledge of a species' range, distribution, population size, preferred habitat, and flight season.

Binoculars

Some binoculars work better than others for dragonfly-watching. The best are ultra-close-focusing (UCF) binoculars, field glasses that can be focused on a subject that is very close at hand. You need binoculars with this particular feature because fairly often you will be able to get very close to a perched dragonfly—closer than you would get to most birds and other watchable wildlife. But dragonflies are small enough that even when you are standing very close, at a distance of a few feet, extra magnification helps you get a better view.

Many makes and models of binoculars—including models that are advertised as "ideal for viewing wildlife"—are *not* close-focusing binoculars. Typical binoculars can focus on a subject no closer than 25 feet away. But it's often possible to get much closer to dragonflies. At 10 feet away, you're not close enough to get a good look at the field marks with your naked eyes, but if you try to use conventional binoculars to get a better look, you won't see a thing.

For dragonfly-watching, your binoculars should give a crisp, clear image when the subject is a mere 4 to 8 feet away. Check for "close-focus distance" in the manufacturer's specifications for the model you are interested in.

What else should you look for in a good pair of binoculars? Waterproof binoculars are a good idea, because dragonflies are found around wet places. Armored binoculars have a resilient coating—usually rubber or leather—that protects them against the inevitable dings and bumps of field use. Coated lenses reduce glare and reflection, and they also gather more light, so that the brightness and contrast of the image are improved.

Two other features to consider are the magnification power and the objective lens diameter. These traits are commonly expressed in the manufacturer's specifications as a pair of numbers, such as 7x36, 8x42, or 10x42. The first number refers to power, or magnification. When you look through 7x binoculars, the subject is magnified 7 times. It looks 7 times bigger than it would to your naked eye. A pair of 10x binoculars is more powerful than 7x binoculars, magnifying an image 10 times.

The second number in the pair refers to the diameter in millimeters of the two objective lenses—the lenses at the end of the binoculars farthest from your eyes. The larger the diameter of the objective lenses, the more light that enters the binoculars. And in general, the more light, the brighter the image you will see.

So 10x42s give you a big image that's nice and bright. Does that mean they are the best binoculars for dragonfly-watching? Not necessarily. The light-gathering advantages of big binoculars are most evident on dull, overcast days, but you'll probably do most of your dragonfly-watching on days when it's bright and sunny. Those big objective lenses can make binoculars heavy, and they can feel like a lead weight around your neck. Furthermore, 10x binoculars can be harder to use than 7x or 8x binoculars. It's hard to hold them steady, and if your hands shake, the effect is magnified. Also, with high-magnification binoculars, you are more likely to lose the dragonfly in that moment when you swing the lenses up in front of your eyes. You have a narrower field of view—you see less of the background around the subject—so it's harder to find the place you are targeting. For the same reason, it's also harder to track a dragonfly in flight with high-magnification binoculars.

The bottom line is that most people prefer 7x or 8x binoculars for dragonfly-watching. But everyone has his or her own personal preference, so try before you buy. You might want to tag along on a field trip with a local drag-onfly club or bird club and ask other people if you may look through their binoculars to see what suits your viewing style.

Catching Dragonflies

A two thousand-year-old Japanese illustration shows a young boy catching dragonflies with a long-handled net. Today, the simple insect net, a device that has changed little over many centuries of use, continues to be an effective tool for studying dragonflies.

Some dragonfly species simply cannot be identified at a distance, even with the best close-focusing binoculars. To make an ID, you have to hold the dragonfly in your hand so you can examine such features as the shape of the genitalia and the pattern of tiny veins in the wings, using a small, handheld 8x or 10x magnifying lens. For many species, these less-obvious traits are the key to identification.

The same kind of net used to catch butterflies works for catching dragon-flies. Catching dragonflies is far less nerve-wracking than catching butterflies, because for the most part, dragonflies are not as fragile as butterflies, which have delicate, scale-coated wings. Usually you can catch a dragonfly in a net, handle it, and release it in fine condition. It's best not to use your net on freshly emerged teneral dragonflies, however. At this stage, a mere touch can damage their still-soft bodies.

Traditional insect nets can vary in design, construction, and cost. A basic net should have a round opening and a lightweight handle, usually made of wood or aluminum. The opening should be 15 to 18 inches in diameter, and the handle should be 3 to 6 feet long. The taller you are, the longer the handle you can get, but with a longer handle, it takes a little longer to swing the net.

The funnel-shaped bag of the net should be twice as long as the diameter of the opening—think of a knee sock rather than an ankle sock. You'll need a good, long net bag to improve the probability of a successful capture. After you swing the net downward and trap the dragonfly inside, you have to give the net a little flip, folding the bag over, to keep the dragonfly from simply fly-ing out of the net. If the net bag is too short, the flip maneuver won't trap the dragonfly inside.

Choose a net with mesh that is small enough to snare a dragonfly, but not so fine that it impedes air flow, which would slow down your swing. Some experienced dragonfly collectors recommend green or black mesh instead of white; the theory is that the dark color blends with the background vegetation and is less conspicuous to keen-eyed dragonflies. This idea hasn't been sys-tematically tested, however. A professional-quality net from a biological sup-ply company costs about $20 to $50. The cheap toy nets sold at shopping-mall nature stores aren't likely to give much satisfaction in the field.

TRADITIONAL METHODS

You don't absolutely need a net to catch dragonflies. In Japan and Korea, people have traditionally captured perched dragonflies using just their bare hands. Here's the time-honored technique: Approach the dragonfly very slowly from the front. When you are a few feet away, start to trace a circle in the air with your index finger. Slowly reduce the diameter of the circle until you are tracing a tiny circle, 1 to 2 inches in diameter. The idea is that the dragonfly becomes mesmerized by your movements and allows you to reach out and pick it up. It's worth a try!

Many dragonflies like to settle on tall perches, and another traditional method of capturing dragonflies capitalized on this habit. The technique involved dabbing the top of a tall pole with something sticky, then carrying the pole out into a rice paddy or some other place where dragonflies are common. Zooming in to perch on the pole, the drag-onflies would get trapped in the goo.

In Japan, catching large dragonflies was once a traditional source of summer amuse-ment for small boys, who used a method called *buri* or *toriko*. They tied two small weights, similar to fishing weights, to either end of a length of lightweight silk cord, about 2 to 3 feet long. Boys would toss the string up in the air just ahead of an airborne dragonfly. The dragonfly might mistake the weights for insect prey, strike at one of them, get tangled in the fine silk cord, and be dragged to the ground by the weights.

Catching dragonflies takes practice. Expect to come up empty-netted on your first few swings. Two factors can work to your advantage in netting dragonflies. For one, dragonflies don't see *quite* as well to the rear as they do to the front. And two, many species have a habit of patrolling back and forth along predictable pathways. Watch to see if the dragonfly is following a pre-dictable flight path. When you think you know where it's likely to go, station yourself in a concealed location, crouching down in tall grass or using a shrub for cover. Hold the net low and still, so it's not conspicuous. Don't swing at the dragonfly when it approaches you—it will certainly see you and perform evasive maneuvers. Instead, wait until it passes right by you, then swing upward at it, from behind. Give the net a little flip to close the opening.

Dragonflies that perch flat on the ground are a little easier to catch than dragonflies in flight. Creep up on the dragonfly from behind, staying low. When you are a few feet away, sit down on the ground. Place the net flat on the ground, and move it slowly forward until it's about a foot from the drag-onfly. Let the net sit motionless for a minute so the dragonfly stops viewing it as a threat. Then quickly lift the net just a few inches, and bring it down over the dragonfly.

To get a dragonfly out of the net so that you can examine it, slide one hand inside the net, using your other hand to hold it closed over your forearm. With your thumb and forefinger or first two fingers, gently pinch the wings together, up over the dragonfly's back. You can hold the dragonfly by the wings this way while you examine it, or you can temporarily release it into a glass jar or plastic bag. Stand in the shade when you do this, and don't keep the dragonfly confined for long.

Although dragonflies do not sting, the big ones may try to bite you. The experience is more startling than painful. Also, females may try to poke you with their sharp ovipositors. Remember that these behaviors are defensive strategies. You're the giant who attacked first.

Where to Find Dragonflies

If you want to see dragonflies, you have to go where the dragonflies are. In general, that means the edges of lakes, ponds, rivers, streams, bogs, marshes, and seeps. The immature adults of many species fly away from water to take refuge in forest habitat until their bodies harden and grow strong, so you can also look for dragonflies along woodland roads and in sunny forest clearings. Even after they are sexually mature, the adults of many dragonfly species forage for insect prey in open fields and meadows, far from water. So check these places too.

Within each of these habitats exist microhabitats—places with slightly different conditions that are particularly attractive to dragonflies. Near bodies of water, check stones and fallen logs along the shore; dragonflies like to bask on the flat, sun-warmed surfaces. Also check the plants growing along the water's edge, scanning slowly and systematically with your binoculars. Damselflies tend to spend more time sitting still than they do flying around, resting semicamouflaged on the shoreline vegetation.

Different dragonfly species lay their eggs in different places, so scan all these places for signs of activity. Some insert their eggs into emergent vegetation such as cattails and bulrushes; others insert their eggs into or stick them on floating or submerged vegetation; and still others lay their eggs in open water.

Males of some species claim and defend territories that they patrol with clockwork regularity. If you've got a canoe or kayak, a quiet paddle close to shore is an excellent way to see these territory holders. Or pull on a pair of rubber boots or fishing waders, and wade slowly along the shoreline or upstream. Along a stream or river, check exposed rocks out in the middle of the current—clubtails often prefer these midstream perches.

If you are looking for dragonflies in a field or meadow, edge habitat—where the field butts up against forest—can be very productive. Insect prey are abundant here, so dragonflies come to these areas to feed.

Bird watchers know that when you drive along a country road, you should check the telephone wires systematically for perched American Kestrels. Dragonflies often behave like kestrels—they'll settle on tall perches where they have a good view of the surrounding terrain to watch for prey, then make sallies from these perches to snag their meals. Scan perch sites such as fencerows and tall weed stems for perching dragonflies such as meadowhawks and pennants.

If you see a dragonfly take flight but have trouble tracking it through your binoculars, try keeping your binoculars trained on the perch that the dragonfly just left—it may return. Or if you spot a stem that looks like a perfect dragonfly perch but is uninhabited, watch it for a while to see if a dragonfly touches down.

When to Go

In general, dragonflies are most active when the weather is warm and sunny. You'll have the best luck on days when the air temperature is 65 degrees Fahrenheit or more. In cold, windy, or rainy weather, dragonflies tend to find sheltered places and hunker down.

To some extent, the time of day can also influence what species you see. Certain species are most active early in the day, others tend to be active at midday, while others are still flying around sunset. Field guides will tell you when to watch for peaks of activity.

How to Get Close

Dragonflies have excellent eyesight and can see you coming. If you've spotted a dragonfly and you'd like to get a closer look, approach slowly, without making any sudden movements. Your best bet, if you can work your way around, is to approach the dragonfly from behind, where it can't see you quite so well.

Notice where the sun is, and don't let your shadow precede you—it could startle the dragonfly from its perch. You don't need to worry about shushing noisy members of your party, however; dragonflies are not startled by loud noises.

6

Attracting Dragonflies to Your Backyard

You can attract dragonflies to your backyard by providing appropriate habitat for both nymphs and adults. To do this, you'll need to create a dragonfly pond and add plants and other dragonfly-friendly features, such as flat rocks for basking and sticks for perching.

A backyard pond will attract dragonflies only if your yard is within a few miles of a lake, pond, stream, or other water source that already supports dragonflies. But don't worry: this description applies to almost every yard in the United States east of the Mississippi River. Wherever you live, there's probably a natural body of water or a farm pond, stormwater detention basin, or wastewater treatment plant within a few miles of your home. All of these places typically support thriving dragonfly populations. And when it's time for the adults to mate and lay eggs, often a few individuals disperse and end up colonizing new places.

The dragonfly species most likely to visit your backyard habitat include strong fliers and species that breed in small ponds. Most of the dragonfly species presented in the field guide section fit this description. The Common Green Darner and Wandering Glider, probably the two most common and widespread dragonflies in all of North America, are both attracted to vernal pools—shallow depressions that fill with water during the spring rains—and both are migratory, so flying far afield is part of their nature. These species are well adapted to finding new habitats. Two other species you're likely to host are the Common Whitetail and the Blue Dasher, both of which typically breed in small ponds and tolerate disturbed conditions.

Your yard might also attract the dragonflies that routinely range far from the water's edge to feed, such as the Yellow Meadowhawk, Twelve-spotted Skimmer, and Common Baskettail. Along with the Common Green Darner and Wandering Glider, these species tend to feed away from open water—over sunny meadows, open fields, even asphalt parking lots.

You probably won't see dragonflies that have specialized habitat needs, such as those whose nymphs develop in streams, rivers, or bogs, unless they wander by because you happen to live close to their habitat.

A dragonfly pond has several key features: underwater habitat, where nymphs can find food and escape from predators; emergent vegetation, where the nymphs can crawl from the water to undergo their transformation into adults; basking sites, where the free-flying adults can get warm in the sun; and perching posts, where dragonflies can sit and scan for food or mates.

If you want a pond that supports dragonflies, don't introduce frogs or ornamental fish such as koi or goldfish—they'll prey on the nymphs. Ducks and other ornamental waterfowl also prey on dragonflies, both the nymphs and the adults.

Making the Pond

The "instant pond" kits—small pond liners made of rigid, preformed plastic or fiberglass—may look easy to install and seem tempting, but they're not your best choice for dragonflies or other wildlife. Preformed ponds tend to be too shallow, too small, and too steep sided to provide appropriate habitat. As far as other pond paraphernalia, although pumps and filters do help maintain water quality, you don't necessarily need them to create a habitat for dragonflies, nor do you need any of the other expensive extras. There are many good resources that give detailed instructions on how to build a backyard pond suitable for dragonflies and many other kinds of wildlife. Several of these are listed in the Resources section at the end of this book.

Pond Location

Put your pond where you can see it—and the dragonflies—from your deck, patio, or a window. Also locate it reasonably close to your outdoor water tap so it's easy to fill.

Watch how the sun moves through your yard, and make sure the location you choose will provide the dragonflies with plenty of sun for basking—it should get at least five or six hours of midday sun. The pond site should also provide the dragonflies with shelter from the prevailing wind. Evergreen trees and shrubs are good wind barriers, or you can use the soil from the pond excavation to build up a gently sloping bank on one side of the pond as a windbreak and basking site. Avoid placing your pond under a deciduous tree, however. Not only will the leaves shade the pond, but when they fall in the water and decay, they can add more nutrients than the system can handle.

Choose a level site. In nature, ponds usually form at the foot of a slope, not at the summit, so if your yard slopes, place the pond at the bottom end—it will look more natural. A heavy rain could cause your pond to overflow, so make sure excess water will drain away from your house, not toward it.

SAFETY FIRST

Small children can drown in a few inches of water. Never allow children to have unsupervised access to your pond. It's a good idea to include a safety fence as part of your landscape design. In fact, a fence may be required by your local safety ordinances. Also check local building ordinances to see if your municipality sets a limit on pond depth.

Pond Size and Depth

The British Dragonfly Society recommends that a dragonfly pond have a minimum surface area of 40 square feet. That translates to a round pond about 7 feet in diameter or an oval pond about 8 feet long and 5 feet wide. Craig Tufts, who is chief naturalist for the National Wildlife Federation and heads up its Backyard Wildlife Habitat program, recommends a 10-foot-diameter pond—large enough to have varying water depths and support diverse plant material. A big pond gives the nymphs places to hide from predators such as raccoons. Dragonflies will still frequent smaller ponds, however, if you don't want or can't afford something that large.

Different dragonfly nymphs prefer different conditions, so the depth of your pond should vary. The more varied the bottom habitat, the wider the variety of dragonfly nymphs that can inhabit the pond.

At its deepest point, your pond should be at least 2 feet deep, or $2\frac{1}{2}$ feet deep if you live where winters are very cold. Deep water buffers the pond from extreme changes in temperatures. A pond that's too shallow can overheat in summer or even dry up completely. In winter, a shallow pond may freeze solid, and that would kill the nymphs overwintering on the bottom. A deep pond will stay liquid year-round and maintain a more stable temperature. Deep areas also provide refuge where nymphs are safe from predators; raccoons won't wade into water much deeper than 18 inches.

Plants for a Dragonfly Habitat

If you're digging your pond in the fall, you can fill it with water right away, but you should wait until spring to put plants in and around your pond. If it's spring or summer, wait a week or two before adding plants. It takes time for the chlorine in municipal water to dissipate. A waiting period also allows any sediment that has washed into your pond from excavation to settle out of the water. Your plants will do better if the water is clear so sunlight can reach them.

Although dragonflies don't require plants as a source of food, aquatic plants are still an important part of their habitat, as are the plants that surround the pond. A good way to decide what plants to put in and around your pond is to pay a visit to a local pond, armed with a field guide to wildflowers and shrubs, and note what plants are growing wild.

Often the plants available in lawn and garden stores are exotic species such as water hyacinth and flowering rush, which are not native to eastern North America. These plants don't have much value for wildlife, and if they escape from the garden into the wild, they can crowd out native species.

It's best to stock your pond with native plants—ones that can be found growing naturally in your region. Don't collect plants from the wild, however. Plants in public parks, refuges, and preserves are often protected under the laws that created the park, even though they are not rare, and collecting plants on private land is trespassing. One way to acquire native plants is to ask for permission to collect plants from a privately owned pond. If you have a friend who has a pond, ask if you can help thin the pondside vegetation. Or you can purchase plants from nurseries that specialize in propagating native species, including some Internet vendors.

Pond plants are typically grouped into categories according to where they grow. Submerged plants are rooted in the bottom of the pond and grow entirely underwater. Some common native species include fanwort and hornwort. Floating plants are not rooted to the bottom; usually their leaves float at or near the surface of the pond. Duckweed is a familiar example. Emergent plants also take root underwater, but the stems and/or leaves poke up above the water. These include water lilies, pondweeds, spatterdock, American lotus, and water shield, all of which grow in deeper water. A fourth category of pond plants might be called marginal or shoreline plants. These are plants that grow well in very wet soil, such as sedges, rushes, arrowhead, pickerelweed, and cattails.

Submerged and floating plants are extremely important components of your pond ecosystem because they add oxygen to the water and remove carbon dioxide. These plants also provide hiding places for dragonfly nymphs, as well as shelter and food for the aquatic organisms that the nymphs prey upon. Your goal is to have about one-third of the pond bottom covered with submerged plants. That doesn't mean you have to plant a whole lot of plants right away; water plants grow quickly and will spread. Floating plants help control the excessive growth of algae in your pond because their leaves shade the water. Aim to have about two-thirds of the water's surface shaded by floating plants. You don't want the plants to be too thick, though. There should still be some open water.

Emergent plants are also important to dragonflies for several reasons. Nymphs crawl up them when it's time to emerge. Emergent plants also serve as perching posts for free-flying adults, providing places to rest, scan for prey, and watch for mates. Also, females of some species need emergent plants as places to lay eggs.

Cattails are one common and widely distributed marginal plant you might be tempted to plant, but they're not recommended for small ponds, as they can spread aggressively. If you still want to plant cattails, be prepared to thin the stands periodically.

Large dragonflies—the species that are most likely to visit a backyard pond—don't use water lilies much, although damselflies and the smaller dragonflies do use flat lily leaves as perch sites. Still, the lilies not only are beautiful, but they also provide habitat for aquatic insects such as fly larvae and water beetles, which are important prey for dragonfly nymphs.

Pickerelweed, a common and widespread marginal, is a great choice for a dragonfly pond, as nymphs often crawl out and emerge on this plant in the wild.

Also give careful thought to the vegetation *around* the pond. There should be a diversity of plant material to provide cover, perching sites for adults, and emerging sites for nymphs. But don't surround your pond exclusively with plants. Landscape the edge with a variety of natural materials, including large rocks, small stones, and gravel, as well as stands of reeds or water-loving shrubs, and perhaps a fallen log as an accent. Also plant some shrubs a few feet away from the water's edge, leaving a little open space at the edge of the water. These will provide additional perching sites.

Basking Sites

Place a few large, flat stones along the sunniest side of the pond to create basking sites. Flagstones are a good choice. Common Whitetails, Eastern Pondhawks, and the meadowhawks are some of the species that especially like to bask on flat surfaces. All of them are attracted to light-colored rocks.

Another way to make a basking site is to position a log or a piece of driftwood at an angle to the edge of the pond, with one end in and one end out of the water. Disrupting the edge this way makes the pond look more natural, and placed in a sunny spot, the wood will serve as a basking site for dragonflies.

Putting some perching sticks in your pond can quickly draw dragonflies, which will use the sticks as territorial posts on which to bask and to survey the territory. Any tall, slender stick can serve as a dragonfly perching post. The green garden stakes made of bamboo or plastic work especially well, although you can use ornamental garden stakes if you prefer. The dragonflies don't care what their perches look like—they just want a good view over the pond.

Insert a few sticks into some of the potted plants in the pond. Vary the heights, adjusting them so that the tip of each stick is 1 to 3 feet above the surface of the water.

Maintaining the Pond

Soon after you fill the pond, algae may spread quickly over the surface; this is called an algal bloom. It's tempting to drain the pond and refill it, but don't— the problem will just repeat itself. Be patient. Your pond will settle down eventually as the algae use up nutrients, die, and sink to the bottom.

If duckweed or other floating plants start to crowd too thickly on the surface of the water, skim off some of the excess growth. Compost this material, just like garden clippings, or give the plants to a friend who is setting up a pond.

It's OK to add some water to your pond if the level starts to get low during a summer dry spell. And it's a good idea to add a bucket of water from a natural pond once a year. The water contains bacteria, zooplankton, and other microorganisms that play important roles in pond ecosystems.

If your pond starts to get choked with fallen leaves in autumn, skim them out; a swimming pool net works well. Check the dead leaves for clinging nymphs before discarding them. You may want to leave them in a container for a few hours or overnight. The nymphs will drop off into the water that collects at the bottom, and you can return them to the pond. Emergent plants around the pond also may hold nymphs, so if you are trimming and thinning these plants, pile the clippings at the water's edge, or on a wide mesh screen or piece of chicken wire positioned with one end resting in the pond. Leave the clippings overnight so the nymphs can drop back into the water.

In nature, ponds fill up with sediment over time and turn back into meadows. To keep your pond a pond, you may need to remove some decayed plant matter from the pond bottom each spring. But don't try to dredge out all the muck—it holds nutrients that your pond ecosystem needs to function.

RESOURCES

Textbooks

Dragonflies of the World, by Jill Silsby. Washington, DC: Smithsonian Institution Press, 2001.

    A scholarly but very readable account of the general behavior and life history of dragonflies, this book has spectacular photographs of odonates in action.

Dragonflies: Behavior and Ecology of Odonata, by Philip S. Corbet. New York: Comstock Publishing Associates, Cornell University Press, 1999.

    Everything you ever wanted to know about dragonfly behavior is in here; be advised, though, the language is pretty technical.

Dragonflies of North America, by James G. Needham, Minter J. Westfall, Jr., and Michael L. May. Gainesville, FL: Scientific Publishers, 2000.

Damselflies of North America, by Minter J. Westfall and Michael L. May, Jr. Gainesville, FL: Scientific Publishers, 1996.

    These two books are manuals or taxonomic keys used by the experts to identify odonates. Together, they cover all the dragonflies and damselflies known to occur in North America. Hundreds of detailed drawings and photomicrographs show minute details of anatomy such as wing venation and genital structure.

An Introduction to the Aquatic Insects of North America, 3rd edition, edited by R.W. Merritt and K.W. Cummins. Dubuque, IA: Kendall-Hunt, 1996.

    For field biologists, this book is a standard. It's useful for identifying a variety of aquatic insects; the Odonata are just one of nine aquatic insect orders covered.

Field Guides: North America

Beginner's Guide to Dragonflies, by Blair Nikula, Jackie Sones, and Donald and Lillian Stokes. New York: Little, Brown and Co., 2002.

    This neat little field guide fits right in your pocket, so it's very handy on field trips. About one hundred of the most common damselflies and dragonflies in North America are covered, and each species is presented on its own page, with a close-up color photograph, range map, and life history information. This guide is very easy to use, with an identification table on the inside front cover that helps you assign dragonflies to their family group, plus a color-tab index so you can navigate through different sections of the guide.

Dragonflies through Binoculars: A Field Guide to Dragonflies of North America, by Sidney W. Dunkle. Oxford: Oxford University Press, 2000.

This is the only field guide available that covers *all* the dragonflies of North America, with detailed and authoritative life history information plus range maps. Every species is depicted with a color photograph, though the images are grouped in a separate section from the life history information, which makes this guide a little tricky for beginners to use. This guide does not cover damselflies, which will be covered in a sequel.

Field Guides: Eastern States

Guides that cover dragonflies throughout North America can be hard for beginners to use because there are so many species to choose from, many of which will never show up at your neighborhood pond. A state field guide makes identification easier because it presents only the species found in your local area. So far, guides are available for just a few states, but the guide for a nearby state should still be pretty useful.

Florida

Dragonflies of the Florida Peninsula, Bermuda, and the Bahamas, by Sidney W. Dunkle. Gainesville, FL: Scientific Publishers, 1989.

Damselflies of the Florida Peninsula, Bermuda, and the Bahamas, by Sidney W. Dunkle. Gainesville, FL: Scientific Publishers, 1990.

Indiana

Dragonflies of Indiana, by James R. Curry. Indianapolis: Indiana Academy of Science, 2001.

Massachusetts

Dragonflies and Damselflies of Cape Cod, by V. Carpenter. Cape Cod Museum of Natural History, Natural History Series 4, 1991.

A Field Guide to the Dragonflies and Damselflies of Massachusetts, by Blair Nikula, Jennifer Loose, and Matthew R. Burne. Westborough, MA: Massachusetts Natural Heritage Program, 2003.

Ohio

Dragonflies and Damselflies of Ohio, edited by Robert Glotzhober and David McShaffney. Ohio Biological Survey, 2002.

Dragonflies and Damselflies of Northeast Ohio, by Larry Rosche. Cleveland: Cleveland Museum of Natural History, 2002.

Wisconsin

A Color Guide to Common Dragonflies of Wisconsin, by Carl and Dorothy Legler and Dave Westover. 429 Franklin St., Sauk City, WI 53583, 1998.

Field Guides: Video

Common Dragonflies of the Northeast, by Richard Walton and Richard Forster. Concord, MA: Brownbag Productions, 1997.

This video is a great way to jump-start your knowledge of dragonflies. Enjoy the live-action footage of more than forty common species, presented in a seasonal parade from spring to summer to fall.

Dragonfly Organizations

These organizations are dedicated to the study of dragonflies and damselflies. Anyone can join them—you don't have to have an advanced degree or make dragonflies your life's work to be a member. Informative publications are a benefit of membership.

Dragonfly Society of the Americas (DSA)

Membership: Attn. Jerrell J. Daigle
2067 Little River Lane
Tallahassee, FL 32311
e-mail: jdaigle@nettally.com
website: www.afn.org/~iori/dsaintro.html

DSA is a nonprofit organization that exists "to encourage scientific research, habitat preservation, and aesthetic enjoyment of odonata." Membership is $15 per year; members receive *Argia*, a quarterly news journal.

World Dragonfly Association (WDA)

Membership: Attn. Dr.Vicky McMillan
Dept. of Biology
Colgate University
13 Oak Drive
Hamilton, NY 13346-1398
website: powell.colgate.edu/wda/dragonfly.htm

This international organization aims to facilitate communication among dragonfly experts worldwide. WDA publishes the scientific journal *Pantala* and the newsletter *Agrion*. Membership is $52 per year with journal and newsletter subscription; $23 per year with newsletter only.

State Odonata Surveys

Regular odonata surveys are conducted in several eastern states to assess the distribution of dragonfly species and population trends. Some of the surveys listed here are run by state wildlife agencies, others by groups of dedicated volunteers. In either case, surveys always need more volunteers who can help.

Maine Dragonfly and Damselfly Survey
Maine Department of Fish and Wildlife
650 State St.
Bangor, ME 04401
phone: 207-941-4239
website: mdds.umf.maine.edu

Michigan Odonata Survey
University of Michigan
Museum of Zoology
Ann Arbor, MI 48109
phone: 734-647-2199
website: insects.ummz.lsa.umich.edu/MICHODO/MOS.html

New Jersey Odonata Survey
website: njodes.com/njos.htm

Ohio Odonata Survey
Jerrell J. Daigle
2067 Little River Lane
Tallahassee, FL 32311
e-mail: jdaigle@nettally.com
website: mcnet.marietta.edu/~odonata/officers.html

Minnesota Dragonfly Monitoring Project
Minnesota Department of Natural Resources Information Center
500 Lafayette Rd.
St. Paul, MN 55155-4040
phone: 651-296-6157 or 888-MINNDNR
website: www.dnr.state.mn.us/ecological_services/nongame/
    projects/dragonfly.html

Rhode Island Odonata Atlas
Rhode Island Natural History Survey
1 Greenhouse Rd., URI
Kingston, RI 02881
phone: 401-874-5800
website: www.rinhs.org

Useful Websites

Digital Dragonflies

www.dragonflies.org/Welcome.html

Photographing dragonflies in the field can be tricky. Forrest L. Mitchell of the Texas Agricultural Experiment Station decided to capture live dragonflies and place them on a flatbed scanner. Voilà: digital dragonflies. OK, they've been posed, but the images are sharp, large, and in focus; the colors are natural; and all the distinguishing field marks are easy to see. The website also tells you how to scan your own specimens without harming them, so if you have access to a scanner, you could create your own archive.

Dragonflies and Damselflies of the United States

www.npwrc.usgs.gov/resource/distr/insects/dfly/dflyusa.htm

The U.S. Geological Survey's Biological Resources Division maintains this website. Click on your state to learn what species are found there, and in what locations.

Ode News

www.odenews.net/images.htm

This is a photographic reference guide to all the dragonflies of North America. Species are grouped by family. The website is maintained by *Ode News*, a newsletter about dragonflies and damselflies in southern New England.

Odonata Information Network

www.afn.org/~iori/

Maintained by the International Odonata Research Institute (IORI), a nonprofit corporation chartered by the state of Florida and located in Gainesville, this web page offers links to many important dragonfly websites.

Web-based Fast Key to North American Dragonflies

www.bio.gasou.edu/bio-home/Harvey/dragonkey.html

Dr. Alan Harvey of Georgia Southern University developed this outstanding web-based key. It's easy to use, and you can identify dragonflies even if you don't know the difference between an anal loop and a hindwing triangle. Capture some specimens, take them home with you, and turn on your computer; this key presents pairs of photographs with the distinguishing features clearly labeled. Just click on the one that most resembles your specimen, and the key guides you through the identification process. Try it!

Insect Nets and Other Entomological Supplies

The following companies are well-known suppliers of field gear for entomologists. Listing here does not imply endorsement of these vendors or their products.

BioQuip Products
17803 LaSalle Ave.
Gardena, CA 90248-3602
phone: 310-324-0620
fax: 310-324-7931
e-mail: bioquip@aol.com
website: www.bioquip.com

Forestry Suppliers Inc.
205 West Rankin St.
P.O. Box 8379
Jackson, MS 39284-8397
phone: 800-647-5368
e-mail: sales@forestry-suppliers.com
website: www.forestry-suppliers.com/

Ward's Natural Science Establishment
P.O. Box 92912
Rochester, NY 14692-9012
phone: 716-359-2502
website: www.wardsci.com

American Biological Supply Co.
2405 N.W. 66th Court
Gainesville, FL 32653-1633
phone: 352-377-3299
fax: 352-375-AMBI

Binoculars

Binoculars 101
www.binoculars101.com/bin-choose-butterfly.html
The Eagle Optics website includes a page on what makes binoculars suitable for butterfly-watching. The advice applies equally well to dragonfly-watching.

Binoculars for Butterflying
www.naba.org/binocs.html
The website of the North American Butterflying Association includes an article by Gary Fellers reviewing close-focusing binoculars.

Birding Optics
http://www.birdwatching.com/optics.html
Many of the binoculars recommended for bird-watching are also suitable for watching dragonflies. The birding.com website also has good information on the newest makes and models.

Birding Resources
http://www.americanbirding.org/resources/
 The American Birding Association website offers good basic information on binoculars.

Backyard Ponds

Here are some good how-to books on pond construction:

The Natural Water Garden: Pools, Ponds, Marshes and Bogs for Backyards Everywhere, edited by C. Colston Burrell. Brooklyn: Brooklyn Botanical Garden, 1997.

The Master Book of the Water Garden: The Ultimate Guide to the Design and Maintenance of the Water Garden, by Philip Swindells. Boston: Bullfinch Press, 2002.

American Horticultural Society Complete Guide to Water Gardening, by Peter Robinson. New York: DK Publishing, 1997.

The Ponder's Bible, by Gosta H. Lovgren. Lavallette, NJ: Carolelle Publishing, 2000.

The following websites have information on pond construction and maintenance:

The National Wildlife Federation's Backyard Wildlife Habitat Program
www.nwf.org/backyardwildlifehabitat/
 For more than thirty years, the National Wildlife Federation has encouraged homeowners to create backyard habitat for wildlife. Click on Tips and Projects for information on backyard ponds.

USDA Natural Resources Conservation Service (NRCS)
www.nrcs.usda.gov/feature/backyard/
 The NRCS helps private landowners conserve soil, water, and natural resources on their properties. This website offers information on creating and maintaining a backyard pond and a backyard wetland.

Biggs Wildlife Pond
www.bigsnestpond.net/
 Kathy Biggs is the author of *Common Dragonflies of California*. This website lets you explore her backyard pond, created expressly for dragonflies.

British Dragonfly Society
www.dragonflysoc.org.uk/
 The useful booklet *Dig a Pond for Dragonflies* can be downloaded from the website of the British Dragonfly Society.